Tents, Temples, and Palaces

A SURVEY OF THE OLD TESTAMENT

by Rick C. Howard

AN INDEPENDENT-STUDY TEXTBOOK

4th edition

Developed in cooperation with
Global University staff

Address of the Global University office in your area:

School for Evangelism and Discipleship
Global University
1211 South Glenstone
Springfield, MO 65804
USA

© 1981, 1995, 2006 Global University
All rights reserved. First edition 1981.
Fourth edition 2006.

Unless otherwise indicated, Scripture is taken from the Holy Bible, NEW INTERNATIONAL VERSION®. Copyright © 1973, 1978, 1984 International Bible Society. All rights reserved throughout the world. Used by permission of International Bible Society.

PN 04.01.11

ISBN 978-0-7617-1146-9

Printed in the United States of America

Table of Contents

	Page
COURSE INTRODUCTION	5

UNIT ONE: *HISTORY OF THE BEGINNINGS*

1. God's Ways and God's Words 14
2. History of the Human Race 34
3. History of the Chosen People 58
4. History of Faith and Worship 82

UNIT TWO: *LIVING IN THE LAND*

5. A Home for the People of God 116
6. A Kingdom United 144
7. Writings of a Kingdom Age 168
8. A Kingdom Divided 186

UNIT THREE: *DESTRUCTION AND REBUILDING*

9. Judgment and Captivity 216
10. Return and Restoration 234

Glossary 254
Answers to Self-Tests 260
Appendix 268
Unit Student Reports 273
Answer Sheets 287
Invitation/response 296

THE GU CHRISTIAN SERVICE PROGRAM

This is one of 18 courses (subjects) that make up the GU Christian Service Program. The symbol at the left is a guide for order of study in the series, which is divided into three units of six courses each. *Tents, Temples, and Palaces: A Survey of the Old Testament* is Course 2 in Unit II. You will benefit by studying the courses in the proper order.

Study materials in the Christian Service Program have been prepared in a self-teaching format especially for Christian workers. These courses provide a student with Bible knowledge and skills needed for practical Christian service. You may study this course in order to receive credit toward a certificate, or for personal enrichment.

ATTENTION

Please read the course introduction very carefully. It is important that you follow these instructions so you can achieve the goals of the course, and be prepared for the student reports.

Address all correspondence concerning the course to your GU instructor at the address stamped on the copyright page near the front of the study guide.

COURSE INTRODUCTION

Learn About the People of God

In this course you will study the Old Testament, the first part of the Holy Bible. The Old Testament tells about the Creator of the heavens and the earth, and of His dealings with the people He chose to use as instruments through whom to bless the world.

The first unit contains an introductory lesson that will help you discover why the Old Testament is a personal message for you. You will find out interesting facts about how it has been preserved and passed on to us. In the remaining lessons of this unit learn about how God created humankind and began to make himself known to them. He called out a special people for himself and delivered them from slavery with mighty miracles. You will learn how He taught them to worship Him.

In the second unit you will become familiar with Palestine, the land God promised to His people. With the help of the maps and charts given you will learn its main characteristics. You will follow God's people as they entered this land, possessed it, and finally took their place among the nations of the world. See also the magnificence and splendor that came upon them when they lived in obedience to God.

In the third unit you will see how God's people were exiled from their land because of their disobedience to Him. It was a time of heartbreaking failure. But God continued to speak to them. He brought them back to their land and inspired them to restore and rebuild what had been destroyed. As you consider this particular time in their history you will learn valuable lessons about the importance of obedience and restoration.

This course will help you understand not only the Old Testament but the New Testament as well, for the New is the fulfillment of the Old. Your study of the history of God's people will strengthen your own knowledge of God's ways and your walk with Him.

Course Description

Tents, Temples, and Palaces gives the student an introduction to the Old Testament. It emphasizes the history of God's people, paying special attention to God's mighty acts and the prophetic words He gave concerning those acts. It deals with the sequence and meaning of the experiences of God's people. It examines their relationship to Him and their successes and failures. The student will discover many truths from the Old Testament that will help him in his understanding of the Bible, his walk with God, and his service for Him.

Course Objectives

When you finish this course you should be able to:

1. Explain why believers today can benefit from studying the Old Testament.
2. Describe the land of Palestine and the major events in the history of the *people of God*.
3. Appreciate the value of the different kinds of writings found in the Old Testament.
4. Apply to your life and teach to others the truths concerning God which are found in the Old Testament.

Textbooks

You will use this independent-study textbook, *Tents, Temples, and Palaces* by Rick C. Howard as both the textbook and study guide for the course. The Bible is the only other textbook required.

Study Time

How much time you actually need to study each lesson depends in part on your knowledge of the subject and the strength of your study skills before you begin the course. The time you spend also depends on the extent to which you follow directions and develop skills necessary for independent study. Plan your study schedule so that you spend enough time to reach the objectives stated by the author of the course and your personal objectives as well.

Lesson Organization and Study Pattern

Each lesson includes: 1) lesson title, 2) opening statement, 3) lesson outline, 4) lesson objectives, 5) learning activities, 6) key words, 7) lesson development including study questions, 8) self-test (at the end of the lesson development), 9) answers to the study questions. Answers to each self-test are at the back of your textbook before the unit student reports.

The lesson outline and objectives will give you an overview of the subject, help you to focus your attention on the most important points as you study, and tell you what you should learn.

Most of the study questions in the lesson development can be answered in spaces provided in this study guide. Longer answers should be written in a notebook. As you write the answers in your notebook, be sure to record the number and title of the lesson. This will help you in your review for the unit student report.

Do not look ahead at the answers until you have given your answer. If you give your own answers, you will remember what you study much better. After you have answered the study questions, check your answers with those given at the end of the lesson. Then correct those you did not answer correctly. The answers are not given in the usual numerical order so that you will not accidentally see the answer to the next question.

These study questions are very important. They will help you to remember the main ideas presented in the lesson and to apply the principles you have learned.

How to Answer Questions

There are different kinds of study questions and self-test questions in this study guide. Below are samples of several types and how to answer them. Specific instructions will be given for other types of questions that may occur.

A *MULTIPLE-CHOICE* question or item asks you to choose an answer from the ones that are given.

1 The Bible has a total of
a) 100 books.
b) 66 books.
c) 27 books.

The correct answer is *b) 66 books*. In your study guide, make a circle around *b)* as shown here:

1 The Bible has a total of
a) 100 books.
(b) 66 books.
c) 27 books.
d) 2 books.

(For some multiple-choice items, more than one answer will be correct. In that case, you would circle the letter in front of each correct answer.)

A TRUE-FALSE question or item asks you to choose which of several statements are TRUE.

Example

2 Which statements below are TRUE?
a) The Bible has a total of 120 books.
(b) The Bible is a message for believers today.
c) All of the Bible authors wrote in the Hebrew language.
(d) The Holy Spirit inspired the writers of the Bible.

Statements **b** and **d** are true. You would make a circle around these two letters to show your choices, as you see above.

A *MATCHING* question or item asks you to match things that go together, such *as* names with descriptions, or Bible books with their authors.

Example

3 Write the number for the leader's name in front of each phrase that describes something he did.

Course Introduction

.**1 a** Received the Law at Mt. Sinai   1) Moses
.**2 b** Led the Israelites across Jordan   2) Joshua
.**2 c** Marched around Jericho
.**1 d** Lived in Pharaoh's court

Phrases a and d refer to Moses, and phrases **b** and **c** refer to Joshua. You would write **1** beside **a** and **d**, and **2** beside **b** and **c**, as you see above.

Ways to Study This Course

If you study this GU course by yourself, all of your work can be completed by mail. Although GU has designed this course for you to study on your own, you may also study it in a group or class. If you do this, the instructor may give you added instructions besides those in the course. If so, be sure to follow his instructions.

Possibly you are interested in using the course in a home Bible study group, in a class at church, or in a Bible school. You will find both the subject content and study methods excellent for these purposes

Unit Student Reports

In the back of your study guide are located the unit student reports and answer sheets. These are to be completed according to the instructions included in the course and in the unit student reports. You should complete and send each unit answer sheet to your instructor for his grading and suggestions regarding your work. Send one when you complete each unit.

Certificate

Upon the successful completion of the course and the final grading of the unit answer sheets by your GU instructor, you will receive your Certificate of Award.

Author of This Course

Rick C. Howard was the pastor of Peninsula Christian Center in Redwood City, California. He was ordained by the Assemblies of God in 1961. He served on the faculty of Northeastern University in Boston, Massachusetts, Evangel College in Springfield, Missouri, and Bethany College in Scotts Valley, California. He also served as National College Youth Representative for the General Council of the Assemblies of God, Springfield, Missouri.

In this course he wrote from much experience as an author, editor, and Bible instructor. Among the books he authored are: *The Judgment Seat of Christ, Strategy For Triumph, The Lost Formula of the Early Church,* and *Songs From Life.* He was also the writer of the GU Christian Service course entitled *Christian Maturity.* In addition, he traveled extensively in many parts of the world as a teacher and preacher.

Mr. Howard earned his B.A. degree at Grove City College in Pennsylvania and his M.A. degree in history at Memphis State University in Memphis, Tennessee.

Your GU Instructor

Your GU instructor will be happy to help you in any way possible. If you have any questions about the course or the unit student reports, please feel free to ask him. If several people want to study this course together, ask about special arrangements for group study.

God bless you as you begin to study *Tents, Temples, and Palaces.* May it enrich your life and Christian service and help you fulfill more effectively your part in the body of Christ.

Additional Helps

Other materials are available for use with this Individual Study Textbook, including supplemental audio cassettes, video cassettes, an Instructor's Guide, and an Instructor's Packet (for instructor's use only). Consult the Evangelism, Discipleship, and Training Manual.

Unit 1

History of the Beginnings

Lessons
1. God's Ways and God's Words
2. History of the Human Race
3. History of the Chosen People
4. History of Faith and Worship

LESSON 1 God's Ways and God's Words

The Old Testament was the first part of the Bible to be written. In its pages is the history of many people who lived over two thousand years ago. Often they faced similar problems that you and I face today, and they reacted in the same way we do. They trusted God, but doubted Him sometimes. They saw His mighty miracles, but needed the assurance of His presence. They were His chosen people, but they often endured severe trials and hardships.

The Old Testament is more than this, though. It was written not only to tell us the stories of these men and women but also to help us understand the nature of God himself. As we study it we will discover how God revealed himself to us in two basic ways: 1) through His mighty works, and 2) through His prophetic messages.

The Old Testament contains many different kinds of writings. Some of these give the history of the nation Israel; some are collections of wise sayings; some are songs of devotion and praise; and others are prophetic messages of great power. Yet in all of them God speaks to us today. As you study this lesson you will learn many facts about the Old Testament and discover that it is a personal message to you.

lesson outline

God Gave Us the Bible
God Speaks Through the Old Testament
Our Approach to the Study of the Old Testament

lesson objectives

When you finish this lesson you should be able to:

- List the three ways God speaks to humans.
- Give evidence to support that the Bible was verbally inspired by God.
- List some facts showing the value, worth, and influence of the Bible.
- State why we should accept the Old Testament as God's Word.
- Explain how the Old Testament was passed on to us.
- Identify the three main divisions of books or writings in the Old Testament.
- State the characteristics of a chronological study of the Old Testament.

learning activities

1. Before starting this lesson, get a notebook. You will use this notebook to write the answers to study questions and exercises when you are told to do so. It can also be used for other notes you desire to make as you study this course.

2. Read the introductory pages in this independent-study textbook carefully. Especially notice the section "How to Answer Questions."

3. Read this opening section including the introductory page, outline, objectives, and learning activities. Find in the glossary at the end of this textbook the definition to any key words that you do not know. Words are valuable and useful.

They help you express your ideas and understand the ideas of others.

4. Carefully read the lesson development, answering each study question as you come to it. As soon as you have answered a question, compare your answer with the one given at the end of the lesson. Then correct your own answer if necessary.

5. Find and read each Scripture referred to in the lesson development as soon as you come to it.

6. When you have completed the lesson, review it. Then answer the questions in the self-test. Check your answers carefully. Review any items you answered incorrectly and learn the correct answers.

key words

A.D.	literature	theme
Aramaic	manuscript	translation
chronological	Masoretes	ultimate
Greek	poetry	vellum
Hebrew	prophecy	verbal
history	revelation	
inspiration	Septuagint	

lesson development

GOD GAVE US THE BIBLE

There are many important things about ourselves that others must tell us. The answers to the questions "Who am I?", "Who are my parents?", and "Where was I born?" cannot just be imagined! In the same way the Bible, God's message to us, deals with the important, ultimate questions about God: What is God like? What has God done in the past and why? And above all, what relationship is there between God and humans? The Bible answers these questions since it is the words and revelation of God himself, the Creator and Redeemer.

The Bible Is God's Message to Us

Objective 1. *List the three ways God speaks to humans.*

God created humans for fellowship with himself. He speaks to us in distinct ways through the voice of nature or creation, and that voice is heard plainly every day (Psalm 19). The apostle Paul affirms that God's eternal power and divine nature are plainly seen in creation (Romans 1:20).

The second way by which God speaks to us is through the Bible, His written Word. The written word has only one theme: the history of God's plan for the redemption of humanity from sin through His son, Jesus Christ.

In the Bible, Jesus Christ is often referred to as the living word of God (John 1:1–18). Therefore, Jesus is the third distinct way in which God has spoken to us (Hebrews 1:2).

Application

1 Read John 1:1–2, 14 and Revelation 19:13. By what name is Jesus Christ revealed and identified in these verses?

. . . .

2 In your notebook, list the three different ways God speaks to us.

The Bible Was Inspired by God

Objective 2. *Give evidence to support that the Bible was verbally inspired by God.*

The name Bible comes from the Greek word biblia which means "many books." The Bible was written by more than 40 authors in many lands over a period of 1400 to 1600 years. The 66 books contained in the Bible were written in several languages and under widely differing circumstances. Yet the Bible is one great book with one great theme. The fact that all these different writings have only one main message is proof that the Bible has its source in God, not in man. Its very existence testifies to this fact. It is a book distinct from all others.

According to 2 Timothy 3:16–17, the Bible was inspired by God. In the language in which they were first written, the words inspired by God actually mean "breathed by God"—His very life. When believers speak of the verbal inspiration of the Bible, they mean that every word of it is God-breathed and is not merely a man's effort to express important truths.

It is true that God miraculously allowed the individual nature of each writer to shine through his writings. Moses, Isaiah, and Samuel, who wrote several of the Old Testament books, were not simply secretaries to whom God dictated His message. Their own personalities are revealed in their writings.

But overall, a sovereign God directed each word in the Scripture. Thus the Bible gives us God's own inspired message. The Bible not only contains the word of God; it is the Word of God. More than 2,000 times in the Old Testament the words the Lord says or similar ones are used (see Exodus 10:3, 11:4, Joshua 24:2, and 2 Samuel 24:12). No other book makes such claims.

Application

3 Circle the letter in front of each statement which is in harmony with the verbal inspiration of the Bible.
- **a)** Though all of the words of the Bible were inspired by God, He allowed the writers to use their own style.
- **b)** Some parts of the Bible were written under more inspiration than others.
- **c)** God chose the thoughts for the Bible writers to express but He did not inspire the words they used.
- **d)** The Bible contains the best thoughts of man expressed in a beautiful and inspiring way.

The Bible Has Great Value and Worth

Objective 3. *List some facts showing the value, worth, and influence of the Bible.*

The first part of the Bible was written more than 3,000 years ago and the last part over 2,000 years ago. Although it was not the first book to be written, it was the first book to be printed when the printing press was invented in 1450 A.D. Now millions of copies are printed each year. Some parts of the Bible have been translated into 2,300 languages, and the whole Bible has been translated into over 300 languages.

The Bible has influenced writers, artists, musicians, and politicians all over the world. They have painted pictures of the events it describes. They have written songs and poems on its themes. They have made laws and changed their societies to conform to the ideals it presents. A great university president once said, "I thoroughly believe in a university education for both men and women; but I believe a knowledge of the Bible without a college course is more valuable than a college course without the Bible."

William Tyndale gave his life so that people in his country of England could read the Bible in their own language. He began to translate the Bible into English in the year 1525. In 1536, with his task incomplete, he was condemned to die for translating the Bible. As he was being burned to death in flames of fire he prayed aloud: "Lord, open the King of England's eyes." What a price Tyndale paid to give the Bible to others!

Application

4 In your notebook, list three facts which show the value, worth, and influence of the Bible.

GOD SPEAKS THROUGH THE OLD TESTAMENT

The Old Testament Is God's Word

Objective 4. *State why we should accept the Old Testament as God's Word.*

You might ask, "Do we have good reason for accepting the Old Testament as the Word of God? One simple way of answering that question with a yes is to point out that Jesus Christ, our Lord and ultimate authority, quoted extensively from it, even validating the use of individual words. Jesus also spoke of and believed in famous Old Testament figures like Adam and Eve, Noah, and Jonah who are routinely dismissed by liberal scholars as mythical. The apostles and other New Testament writers quoted widely from the Old Testament too.

These facts show us that Jesus and the writers of the New Testament valued the Old Testament and recognized its authority. In the Bible, the Old Testament is often referred to as "the Scriptures" and "the Law"—meaning the commandments that God gave to His people. When we find these terms in the New Testament, then, we can usually take them to mean what we call the Old Testament. Today we use the term "Scriptures" also, but our meaning includes the whole Bible or specific verses or portions of it. It is important to keep these different usages in mind when studying and reading the Bible.

Application

5 In your notebook, write a short description of what each Scripture listed below tells about the Old Testament or how it was used.
a) Matthew 22:29, 43–45
b) Luke 24:25–27
c) John 10:34–35
d) 2 Timothy 3:16
e) 2 Peter 1:20–21

The Old Testament tells many historical facts about the Jewish nation. But it is more than just history. It is a sacred history that tells of God's revealing himself to us. The Old Testament shows how God worked with the nation of Israel. However, God is not only the God of Israel but also the supreme ruler of all people everywhere. The following truth is very important: The basic theme of the Old Testament is God revealing His nature to humankind through mighty acts and prophetic words.

The written record of the Old Testament as it was received by Jews and Christians was considered to be a divine-human product, free of error. What is more, it contains truth for the entire human race.

Application

6 Read 1 Thessalonians 2:13. Notice that Paul gives thanks to God for the Thessalonians because they accepted the message as God's message, not man's. What attitude does this suggest that we should have towards the Old Testament?

7 Circle the letter of each statement that gives a reason why we should accept the Old Testament as God's message. (Note: all of the statements are true, but not all of them give reasons.)
a) It tells us many historical facts.
b) The writings of many different men are contained in it.
c) Jesus said that its words are true forever.
d) None of it came simply by the will of man.

We Can Rely on the Old Testament

Objective 5. *Explain how the Old Testament was passed on to us.*

From earliest times God has caused men to keep a written account of His words and revelations. The kings of Israel were to have a copy of His law (Deuteronomy 17:18–19). Most of the Old Testament is written in Hebrew, the language spoken by the people of Israel until about 500 years before Christ. At that time Aramaic became the common language of Palestine and the surrounding countries. A small portion of the Old Testament was written in Aramaic (Ezra 4:8–6:18; 7:12–20; Jeremiah 10:11; and Daniel 2:4–7:28).

The material on which the Old Testament was written was called vellum. Skins of animals were used to prepare this substance. A piece of vellum on which the Scriptures were written usually measured about 10 inches in width and 30 feet in length. These strips were rolled up to form what is called a scroll. When a scroll became worn out through use, a particular group of scholars called Masoretes copied the texts onto a new scroll with great care. The old scroll usually was destroyed. We have manuscripts of this type from around 900 A.D.

However, the discovery of some much earlier manuscripts from around 70 A.D. was made in 1947 at a place called Qumran near the Dead Sea. These manuscripts are called the "Dead Sea Scrolls." They show that the Old Testament which we have received has been faithfully passed on to us. It deserves our wholehearted trust and acceptance!

Many translations of the Old Testament have been made. In the last centuries before Christ, Jewish scholars made a translation into Greek. Tradition says there were 72 translators. Thus the title *Septuagint*, a Greek word meaning seventy, was given to this translation. This made it possible for many more people to read the Old Testament. Along with the Hebrew Old Testament, the Septuagint was used during the time of Jesus' earthly ministry.

In the latter part of the 4th century A.D. a translation was made into Latin by a scholar named Jerome. Then in the

14th and 15th centuries several other translations appeared in German, French, Italian, and English. After the time of William Tyndale, the famous "authorized" or King James Version appeared in 1611. In our day, many other translations have been made. The Bible is now available in the languages of people who live all over the world.

Application

8 Which sentences correctly describe how the Old Testament was passed on to us?
a) The first translation of the Old Testament into a language other than Hebrew was made in the 4th century A.D. English versions today are copies of this translation.
b) The Old Testament was first written on vellum scrolls in the days of Jesus' earthly ministry. The copies that we have today were made from the Septuagint, a Greek version.
c) From earliest times God's words and revelations were recorded in writing. These writings were faithfully preserved, copied, and passed down to us by faithful scholars.

The Old Testament Is a Personal Message to Us

Abraham was the great man of faith who was the father of the nation of Israel. But he was the father of not just that nation. According to Romans 4:11, 16, and 24, believers today are his spiritual descendants. It is this fact which gives the Old Testament meaning to us. It is not only the revelation of God's ways and words, but also the story of our spiritual ancestors and forefathers. Although our circumstances today are different, the spiritual lessons they learned apply to our lives as well.

Hebrews 4:12 notes, "For the word of God is living and active. Sharper than any double-edged sword, it penetrates even to dividing soul and spirit, joints and marrow; it judges the thoughts and attitudes of the heart." Because the Old

Testament is the Word of God it gives us insight not only into His nature but also into ours. As we study the events it records we can discover many things about our own lives. Often we find ourselves in situations similar to the ones encountered by the men and women of the Old Testament. God can speak to us today through our study of their lives and the messages He had for them.

Application

9 In your notebook, describe two ways in which the Old Testament is a personal message to us.

OUR APPROACH TO THE STUDY OF THE OLD TESTAMENT

The Writings in the Old Testament

Objective 6. *Identify the three main divisions of books or writings in the Old Testament.*

Of the 66 books of the Bible, 39 make up the Old Testament. Further, the 39 books of the Old Testament can be divided into three groups. The first 17 books, Genesis through Esther, account for Israel's historical development as a nation until about 500 years before Christ came to earth. These are called the books of history.

The first five books of history were closely associated with the life and ministry of Moses, who led the Israelites out of Egypt: Genesis, Exodus, Leviticus, Numbers, and Deuteronomy. This group of books is often referred to as the Pentateuch, a Greek name meaning "five vessels."

Five books—Job, Psalms, Proverbs, Ecclesiastes, and the Song of Solomon—are called the books of poetry. They express the feelings, thoughts, and emotions of various people who lived during Israel's history. But they are not closely tied to particular events of it.

The remaining 17 books are called the books of prophecy. God raised up prophets from time to time to declare His word. They had a message for their own generation, but they often spoke of future events also. Details in the historical books are the keys to a proper understanding of the message of the prophets. On the other hand, the words of the prophets help the reader to understand what is in the books of history. Chart 1 on the following page shows the arrangement of the Old Testament books in each of these three divisions.

Application

10 Match each verse (left side) to the division of the Old Testament whose type of content it best represents (right side).

... **a** "I love the Lord, for he heard my voice; he heard my cry for mercy" (Psalm 116:1).

1) History
2) Poetry
3) Prophecy

... **b** "Afterward, I will pour out my Spirit on all people. Your sons and your daughters will prophesy" (Joel 2:28).

... **c** "Josiah removed . . . all the shrines at the high places that the kings of Israel had built" (2 Kings 23:19).

... **d** "On the tenth day of the first month, the people went up from the Jordan and camped at Gilgal on the eastern border of Jericho" (Joshua 4:19).

CHART 1: THE DIVISIONS OF THE OLD TESTAMENT		
History	*Poetry*	*Prophecy*
Genesis	Job	Isaiah
Exodus	Psalms	Jeremiah
Leviticus	Proverbs	Lamentations
Numbers	Ecclesiastes	Ezekiel
Deuteronomy	Song of Solomon	Daniel
Joshua		Hosea
Judges		Joel
Ruth		Amos
1 Samuel		Obadiah
2 Samuel		Jonah
1 Kings		Micah
2 Kings		Nahum
1 Chronicles		Habakkuk
2 Chronicles		Zephaniah
Ezra		Haggai
Nehemiah		Zechariah
Esther		Malachi

Chronological Study of the Old Testament

Objective 7. *State the characteristics of a chronological study of the Old Testament.*

For the purpose of this Old Testament survey course we will study the books of history, poetry, and prophecy in what is called a chronological order. That is, the order of our study will follow the actual period of time each book is about. We will begin with the book that tells about the first or earliest events, and end with the book that tells about the last or latest events.

We have seen that the basic theme of the Old Testament is God's revelation of His nature through historical events. But these events, though they were guided by God, could not give us a revelation of His nature by themselves. So God raised up men not only to see those events but also to explain what they revealed about God. These men were the prophets. The seeing and telling of the revelation of God was the task of the prophet. For this course we will study the prophets along with the events they saw and spoke about. We will study the books of poetry along with the period of time during which they were probably written. Chart 2 shows the chronological order that we will follow in our study of the Old Testament.

CHART 2: CHRONOLOGICAL ORDER FOR OUR STUDY

UNIT 1; Lessons 2–4: History of the Beginnings

HISTORY

Genesis   (the Pentateuch)
Exodus
Leviticus
Numbers
Deuteronomy

UNIT 2; Lessons 5–8: Living in the Land

HISTORY	**POETRY**
Joshua	Job
Judges	
Ruth	
1 Samuel	
United Kingdom:	
1 and 2 Samuel	Psalms
1 and 2 Kings	Proverbs
1 and 2 Chronicles	Ecclesiastes
	Song of Solomon

HISTORY		**PROPHECY**	
Divided Kingdom:			
1 Kings 11–12	Jonah	Isaiah	Jeremiah
2 Kings	Hosea	Micah	Lamentations
2 Chronicles	Amos	Nahum	Habakkuk
	Joel	Zephaniah	Obadiah

UNIT 3; Lessons 9–10: Destruction and Rebuilding

Captivity:	Ezekiel
2 Kings 17:4–18	Daniel
Psalm 137	
Esther	
Restoration:	
Ezra	Haggai
Nehemiah	Zechariah
	Malachi

Application

11 Circle the letter in front of each statement which is TRUE about a chronological study of the Old Testament.
- **a)** All the books of prophecy are studied as a group before the books of history are studied.
- **b)** It is the time period which a book covers that is important in a chronological study.
- **c)** The book of Amos is studied before the book of Daniel.

The words of Micah 4:2 provides a beautiful theme as we begin our study of the Old Testament: "Let us go up to the mountain of the LORD, to the house of the God of Jacob. He will teach us his ways, so that we may walk in his paths."

As you study the Old Testament, expect God to speak to you through it. It is a personal message for you!

self-test

After you have reviewed this lesson, take the self-test. Then check your answers with those given in the back of the study guide. Review any questions answered incorrectly.

1 An example of God speaking to us through the written word is the
a) miracle Jesus performed when raising Lazarus from the dead.
b) existence of many forms of life which show God's power.
c) book of Psalms in the Bible.

2 When we say that the Bible was inspired by God we mean that it was
a) breathed by God.
b) written by dynamic men.
c) dictated word by word.

3 Because the Bible was verbally inspired by God
a) all of the writers had the same style.
b) human personalities are not seen in it.
c) it is trustworthy and true throughout.

4 Circle the letter of each TRUE statement below.
a) Because the Old Testament tells about the nation of Israel, it is of little interest to believers today.
b) The men who wrote the Old Testament books of history were not as fully inspired as those who wrote the books of prophecy.
c) Jesus and the writers of the New Testament accepted and relied on the Old Testament as God's Word.
d) In the New Testament, the word "Scripture" usually has reference to the Old Testament.

5 The writings of the Old Testament which are called the books of poetry have as their main subject the
a) story of the sequence of events in the history of God's people.
b) message God gave concerning present and future events.
c) record of the emotions and feelings of God's people.

6 Suppose there are three books called Book A, Book B, and Book C. Read their descriptions given below and choose the one which would be studied first in a chronological study.
a) Book A, which was written before books B and C
b) Book B, which tells about events that happened before those described in both Book A and Book C
c) Book C, which tells about events that happened after those described in Book B

7 Circle the letter in front of each fact which shows that the Old Testament was faithfully passed on to us.
a) The Masoretes were careful scholars who made accurate copies of the Scriptures.
b) The Septuagint was a Greek version used during the days when Jesus was on earth.
c) The Dead Sea Scrolls from 70 A.D. agree with the Old Testament manuscripts from 900 A.D.
d) Hebrew was spoken in Palestine until about 500 years before Christ.

8 Circle the letter in front of each statement which indicates that the Old Testament is a personal message to us.
a) The Old Testament was written over a period of 1400–1600 years.
b) Romans 4:11, 16, and 24 say that we are the spiritual descendants of Abraham.
c) The Old Testament contains 37 books divided into the three divisions of history, poetry, and prophecy.
d) The entire Bible, including the Old Testament, is the Word of God.

Answers To Study Questions

Note: The answers to questions have been given in mixed order. This is done so that you will not see the answer to your next question until you have answered that question.

1 He is called the "Word" and the "Word of God."

7 c) Jesus said that its words are true forever.
d) None of it came simply by the will of man.

2 God speaks to us through a) nature or creation, b) His written word the Bible, and c) Jesus Christ.

8 c) From earliest times God's words and revelations were recorded in writing. These writings were faithfully preserved, copied, and passed down to us by careful scholars.

3 a) Though all of the words of the Bible were inspired by God, He allowed the writers to use their own style.

9 The Old Testament is a personal message to us because: 1) It is the record of our own spiritual forefathers since we are Abraham's spiritual descendants; and 2) it is God's word and as such it gives us insight into our own hearts. (Your answer should be similar.)

4 Your answer could list any of the facts given in the section, such as: it was the first book to be printed, parts of it have been translated into over 2,300 languages, it has had great influence on people's lives, and so forth.

10 a 2) Poetry (Psalm 116:1)
  b 3) Prophecy (Joel 2:28)
  c 1) History (2 Kings 23:19)
  d 1) History (Joshua 4:19)

5 a Jesus said the Sadducees were wrong because they did not know the Scriptures. Jesus used the Scriptures in talking with the Pharisees.
  b The Scriptures speak about Christ, for He explained what they said about Him.
  c What the Scriptures say is true forever.
  d All Scripture is inspired by God.
  e Scripture did not come just from man's will but from God by His Spirit.

(Your answers should be similar.)

11 **b)** and **c)** are true

6 We should treat it with respect as God's message, not man's.

For Your Notes

LESSON 2: History of the Human Race

In the opening pages of Genesis God has given us a record of the beginning of the world, the universe, and everything that these contain. The events described are of great interest and significance to people everywhere, and they have had far-reaching consequences for all humanity.

This lesson deals with material from chapters 1–11 of Genesis. In these chapters we meet some of the most important characters and personalities of the Bible: Adam, Eve, Satan, Noah, Shem, and Abraham. We read, too, about some of the most fateful events of human history: the creation of man and his fall into sin, the destruction of the sinful human race by the Flood, and the selection of a godly family through whom God would bring about His purpose for humankind.

As you study this lesson you will learn about these characters and events and find answers to many questions about the origin of the world and of the people of God, to whom we belong.

History of the Human Race

lesson outline

Beginnings in Genesis
The Great Human Tragedy

lesson objectives

When you finish this lesson you should be able to:

- Tell of various beginnings described in Genesis.
- Identify truths concerning the revelation of God shown in Genesis.
- Describe God's original purpose for humanity.
- Discuss the impact of the Fall.
- State the spiritual lessons seen in the lives of Cain, Abel, and Seth.
- Indicate truths concerning the Flood.
- Identify facts associated with the settlement of Noah's descendants.

learning activities

1. Read Genesis 1–11 in your Bible.
2. Study each part of the lesson development, answering the questions and checking your answers. Be sure to pay special attention to the maps and diagrams given. Take the self-test and check your answers.

key words

altar	crucial	origin
civilization	fertile crescent	redemption
covenant	geographical	

lesson development

BEGINNINGS IN GENESIS

Objective 1. *Tell of various beginnings described in Genesis.*

Genesis is a Greek word meaning "beginning or origin." It is certainly a suitable name for the first book of the Bible, for the book of Genesis tells us of the beginning of everything except God himself who is without beginning or end. Genesis satisfies humanity's natural curiosity about the past and how the world came to be. As Christians we accept its record as the only authentic account of God's creation of the universe and His purpose for it. The further revelation of God to man is built upon the foundation formed by the events and truths it records. There are, for example, more than 60 quotations from Genesis in 17 different books of the New Testament.

Application

1 Match the following Scripture portions (left side) to the beginning each one describes (right side).

... **a** Genesis 1:1–25
... **b** Genesis 1:26–31
... **c** Genesis 3:1–7
... **d** Genesis 3:8–24
... **e** Genesis 4:1–15
... **f** Genesis 4:16–9:29
... **g** Genesis 10–11

1) Family
2) Nations of the world
3) World
4) Civilization
5) Human race
6) Sin
7) Redemption

The Genesis God

Objective 2. *Identify truths concerning the revelation of God shown in Genesis.*

Genesis 1:1 says, "In the beginning God . . ." Who then is God? In Genesis He reveals himself as the divine Creator, the one who has always existed from eternity to eternity. He has no beginning of days nor end of life. And although He created all things, He exists separate from all things. The trees are God's handiwork, but God is not a tree. God created the sun, but the sun is not God.

Application

2 Circle the letter in front of each TRUE statement.
a) Genesis tells us about God's beginning.
b) The creation is separate from God.
c) God is shown in Genesis as the Creator.

The Genesis Event

Three times in Genesis 1 the word create appears (1:1, 27). This word is used to translate a Hebrew word which means to "make something out of nothing." The fact that God made the world out of nothing is an indication that He has all power. When we understand this idea we have taken the first important step towards understanding our relationship to God. The Bible teaches us that it is by faith that we can know God created the world. Hebrews 11:3 says, "By faith we understand that the universe was formed at God's command, so that what is seen was not made out of what was visible."

This belief in God's Word is the basis of a person's relationship to God and of his or her Christian experience. Without such faith it is impossible to please God (Hebrews 11:6). As Christians, we must rely on God's Word, not on our frail and partial human knowledge.

It is far more important to understand that God created everything than to have an opinion on exactly where or when the events of creation took place. The author of Genesis, for example, gives no timetable for the events. He does not suggest a date. Neither does he give exact geographical details about the garden of Eden, man's first dwelling place. These matters are not dealt with. Nevertheless, the important central truth is clear: God created the world from nothing, and His work of creation was characterized by purpose, design, and order. This truth is the foundation and background for the rest of God's revelation which is gradually unfolded in the Bible.

Application

3 The importance of the Genesis account of creation is that it states
a) the date when God created the world.
b) God created the world by His word.
c) exact geographical details about Eden.

Man—God's Masterpiece

Objective 3. *Describe God's original purpose for humanity.*

After giving an account of the origin of the heavens and the earth, the opening chapters of Genesis quickly move to a description of man. Man is clearly the most important being of God's entire creation. Made in the very image or likeness of God, he becomes the center of interest in the revelation of God's purpose.

Man was given both responsibility for and power over creation. God intended that man should rule it (Genesis 1:26, 28). He placed man in a garden in Eden. Man was different from the animals. This difference is made clear by the events described in Genesis 2:18–23. Man could find no satisfactory companion until God created Eve from Adam's own body. This was perfection—an animal and plant kingdom in perfect harmony with humanity. And God was very pleased!

History of the Human Race 39

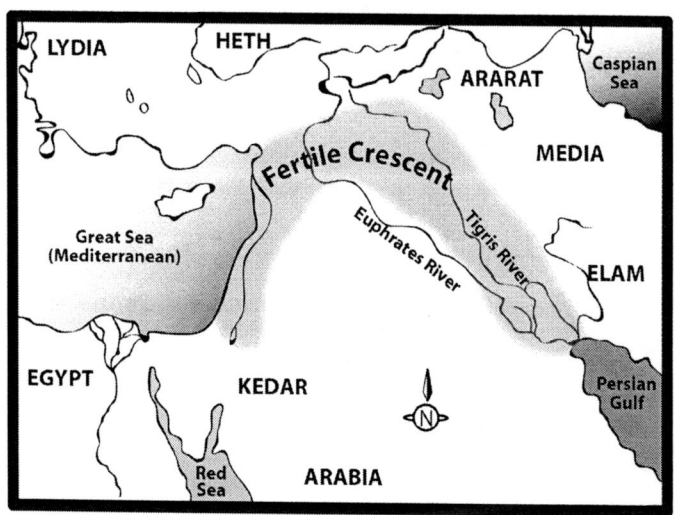

Application

4 Read Genesis 2:10–14. On the map above, find the rivers that are mentioned. Notice the shaded areas. This is called the fertile crescent because of its shape and suitability for growing crops. Many people who study history, including non-Christians, believe that life began there. Circle the letter of each statement following that is TRUE.
a) Ararat is north of the fertile crescent.
b) Only one of the rivers named in Genesis 2:10–14 is near the fertile crescent.
c) There are non-Christians who believe that life began in the area called the fertile crescent.

God wanted man to rule over creation, but He also wanted him to have fellowship with Him. There was perfect order in creation, but within man's being was a powerful force—his will. Initially, the first two humans, Adam and Eve, chose to have fellowship with their Creator (Genesis 3:8). What a wonderful time that must have been! But for humans and God to have true, lasting fellowship, people must freely choose it.

God had given humans freedom of choice. He wanted people to love Him because they chose to do so. The rest of creation—the stars, the sun, the trees—has no freedom of choice. It must move according to its design. But God wanted human beings to freely choose to do His will and to delight in doing so.

Application

5 In your notebook, describe God's two main purposes for humankind. Write one short sentence for each description.

THE GREAT HUMAN TRAGEDY

The Fall and Its Shadow

Objective 4. *Discuss the impact of the Fall.*

Adam and Eve's disobedience, which is described in Genesis 3:1–7, is referred to as the Fall. We have already found out what God's original purpose was for humankind. It was from this height that humans fell.

As the events of Genesis 3 unfold we find Adam and Eve in the Garden. They had complete freedom of choice. But there was another personality present also—Satan. He too had been created for a high purpose. But he had rebelled against God and lost his place (Luke 10:18), and now he attempted to cause God's plan to fail, to draw humans into his own rebellion. He tempted Adam and Eve to use their self-will against God's will. The specific issue was God's command concerning a tree in the midst of the Garden.

Application

6 Read Genesis 2:8–17. In your notebook, answer the following questions.
a) How was the tree described?
b) What was God's command concerning it?

Do not think it strange that the only test involved a tree and fruit. God often tests our obedience by using simple, everyday things. Satan came to Eve in the form of a serpent. Both Adam and Eve failed the test. This failure and disobedience brought about the most crucial change in man's relationship to God. It is the most tragic event in the history of the human race and is referred to repeatedly throughout the Bible (see Romans 5:12, 18–19).

Application

7 Read Genesis 3:1–24. Put the events below in order by numbering them from 1 to 6. Write 1 before the event that happened first, 2 before the event that happened next, and so forth.

... **a** Eve listened to Satan and disobeyed God's command.

... **b** God gave Adam and Eve a command about the tree.

... **c** Adam and Eve were sent out of the Garden.

... **d** Adam ate of the fruit which was forbidden.

... **e** Adam and Eve tried to cover themselves.

... **f** God provided a covering for Adam and Eve.

Let us take a closer look at what actually happened when Adam and Eve sinned. Their action is an example of a pattern we find in the New Testament. This pattern is that we try in the wrong way to satisfy three normal desires God has given us: the desire to possess things, enjoy things, and achieve or attain. In 1 John 2:16 the satisfaction of these three desires outside of God's will is identified as 1) what the sinful self desires, 2) what people see and want, and 3) worldly pride or boasting.

Application

8 Write the phrase from Genesis 3:6 which corresponds to each of these desires below the description of it.

a) Possess things: what the sinful self desires

....

b) Enjoy things: what people see and want

....

c) Achieve or attain: worldly pride or boasting

....

And so our first parents joined Satan in rebellion against God's commands. Immediately, they became conscious of themselves and of their being lost. So they hid from God's holy presence and used leaves to cover their nakedness (Genesis 3:7). The Lord God, later, killed an animal and made clothes from the animal skins for them.

Adam and Eve's spiritual life died as God had said, and their physical bodies came under the threat of death. They were cut off from God—orphaned. Thus, the first humans chose to step down from God's fellowship to Satan's control. From the height of God's purpose they fell into the depths of bondage.

Application

9 Read Psalm 8:4–9 and Hebrews 2:8. Circle the letter in front of each TRUE statement below.
a) God's purpose was for humankind to rule all things.
b) Man is ruler over all things now.
c) All human beings are fulfilling God's purpose today.

God judged everyone who participated in the Fall. The serpent was judged above all animals (Genesis 3:14). Women and men were made subject to suffering, hard toil, and physical death. The story ends with the first humans being exiled from the blissful Garden (Genesis 3:22–24).

History of the Human Race

When God gave humans freedom of choice, He knew there was a danger that every person would turn from good to evil. But though He knew the ultimate possibilities, He still chose that path. Some people have been tempted to wonder if God's purpose has failed, for they look at a world filled with the consequences of sin. But God's plans cannot fail (Isaiah 46:10). He would have never created the world if the gain of His salvation would not far surpass the loss brought about by people's disobedience. God saw that some would make a deliberate choice to reject His deliverance. This truth convinces us of how wonderful the future will be for those who do accept His salvation.

God promised ultimate victory through the woman's offspring (Genesis 3:15). This was a prophecy about Christ, who would come to redeem humanity. Isn't it wonderful that the Christian who overcomes will one day eat of that tree of life? Revelation 2:7 tells us that "the right to eat from the tree of life, which is in the paradise of God" will be given to those who win the victory. What a promise this is to those who choose to live for God and refuse to follow the advice of Satan or to join in his rebellion!

The apostle Paul writes "Oh, the depth of the riches of the wisdom and knowledge of God! How unsearchable his judgments?" (Romans 11:33). God's purposes will not be defeated. One day uncountable multitudes from every nation, people, and language, will sing the song of salvation (Revelation 7:9–12). The eternal purpose of the true God will come to pass!

Application

10 Circle the letter in front of each statement which describes a result of Adam and Eve's disobedience.
a) Adam and Eve continued to have close fellowship with God.
b) Mankind was subjected to physical death.
c) Adam and Eve were exiled from the Garden.
d) God's purpose for humankind failed.
e) Adam and Eve were not allowed to eat of the tree of life.

Descendants and Destruction

Cain, Abel, and Seth

Objective 5. *State the spiritual lessons seen in the lives of Cain, Abel, and Seth.*

Adam and Eve had three sons mentioned in the Bible by name—Cain, Abel, and Seth. The story of Cain and Abel given in Genesis 4 particularly illustrates the condition of humankind following Adam and Eve's sin. Both Cain and Abel worshipped God by bringing an offering. Abel's animal sacrifice was accepted by God, but Cain's offering of vegetable produce was rejected.

These offerings by Cain and Abel early in Bible history echoed the experience of their parents, Adam and Eve. As Adam and Eve had tried to clothe their nakedness and sin by their own efforts, so Cain brought an offering to God of his own works. And as the Lord killed an animal and made coverings for Adam and Eve, so Abel brought an animal sacrifice. In these early events God revealed an important principle: To cover sin there must be blood shed, either death of the sinner or death of a substitute for the sinner.

From Adam, Cain, and onwards, God points forward to the cross of Jesus Christ, for God made it clear that the Savior who had been promised would have to die to pay the penalty for humanity's sins. Every animal sacrifice in the Old Testament pointed ahead to Jesus as the true lamb of God (John 1:29). The sacrifices pictured the death Jesus would suffer to remove sin.

Cain and Abel represent possible attitudes of two groups of people. One group sees no need for a Savior. They feel sufficient in their own goodness. The other group knows that they will be lost unless they accept the sacrifice God has provided for their sin and trust Him for their salvation.

Application

11 God accepted Abel's sacrifice but rejected Cain's. In your notebook, describe in your own words the spiritual principle this teaches us.

Cain displayed an attitude of deliberate disobedience since God had warned him that sin would try to master him (Genesis 4:7). He murdered his brother Abel (Genesis 4:8) and was driven off the land away from the Lord's presence (Genesis 4:14).

Genesis 4:17–24 describes the history of Cain and his descendants. They built cities, made tools, and raised livestock. This was the beginning of civilization. The events and the activities described in these verses took place over a long period of time. The civilization which was developed provided a false sense of security, as shown by the boast of Lamech (Genesis 4:23–24), one of Cain's descendants.

While Cain and his descendants were building their civilization, Adam and Eve had another son of whom Eve said, "'God has granted me another child in place of Abel, since Cain killed him'" (Genesis 4:25). Abel was a godly man. If he had lived, one of his descendants may have been the Savior God had promised. His murder was Satan's attempt to destroy this possibility. But God gave Adam and Eve another son, Seth, through whom God would fulfill His promise. During the lifetime of Seth's son, Enosh, people began to worship using the Lord's name (Genesis 4:26).

For God's plan of redemption to be carried out, there had to be a human line of ancestry from which the Savior could come. It was necessary for God to become a man so He could offer His life in payment to restore humanity's broken relationship with himself. Seth proved worthy to head this line of ancestors of the coming Savior.

Application

12 The importance of Seth in God's plan to restore humanity's broken relationship with Him is that Seth
a) did not experience death.
b) was to be Christ's human ancestor.
c) could pay for man's sin.

13 Compare Genesis 5 to Luke 3:36–38. Eleven of Jesus' earthly ancestors are mentioned in both these passages, counting the ones from Adam to Shem. In your notebook, write down the names of these ancestors in order. Begin with Adam as number 1, and end with Shem as number 11.

The Flood

Objective 6. *Indicate truths concerning the Flood.*

In your list of Jesus' earthly ancestors you named Enoch. Notice how his life is described in Genesis 5:21–24. Compare this description to the one in Hebrews 11:5–6. Enoch did not experience death! He lived in fellowship with God and his life had a special ending. God took him away!

The grandson of Enoch was named Lamech, and Lamech's son was Noah. During Noah's days godlessness increased as violence, wickedness, and corruption abounded. God determined to destroy all the wicked. But God was pleased with Noah. For 120 years God warned everyone through Noah that He was going to destroy the world with a flood. Still only Noah found favor in God's eyes and kept an acceptable relationship with Him.

God commanded Noah to build a large *ark*. Noah obeyed, building it to the exact proportions God gave him. Scientists today would agree that a boat like the one Noah built would be seaworthy and would have room enough for all the life that was to be spared. In building the ark, Noah exercised faith in the words of God. Hebrews 11:7 says, "By faith, Noah when warned of things not yet seen, in holy fear built an ark to save his family."

Noah, his wife, his three sons and their wives, and a representation of every kind of animal and bird life went into the ark as God had commanded. God then sent the Flood. The world was judged by God, and the sinful human race was destroyed. For about a year, Noah and his family and all of the creatures that had been saved had to stay in the ark. Then the waters receded and humankind faced a new opportunity.

Application

14 Read the account of the Flood in Genesis 6–8. Then circle the letter in front of each TRUE statement below.
a) It was by faith that Noah believed God's warning.
b) Noah tried to change God's mind regarding the flood.
c) Noah showed his faith in God by building the ark.

Beginning Again

Objective 7. *Identify facts associated with the settlement of Noah's descendants.*

Noah began the new civilization by building an altar and offering many sacrifices. God then made a covenant or promise with Noah concerning the future of His relationship with humankind. God's action shows us what was His ultimate purpose for judging the world—to restore its relationship with Him.

Application

15 Read Genesis 9 and answer these questions in your notebook.
a) What was God's promise (vv. 8–11)?
b) What was God's sign (vv. 12–17)?

After Noah and his family became settled in the land an incident occurred which is described in Genesis 9:20–27. This incident shows us that even a righteous man like Noah could be tempted and sin. It also reveals the character of Noah's three sons: Shem, Ham, and Japheth. Ham treated his father with disrespect, while Shem and Japheth acted in respect. It was upon Canaan, Ham's son, that the curse of Noah's prophecy fell (vv. 25–27). Centuries later the united Canaanites received terrible judgment when the Israelites occupied their land.

Genesis 10:1–32 is a description of where the descendants of Noah's sons settled. Today, scientists who study the history of humans are finding more evidences that this description is correct. It is the only adequate explanation we have of how people came to live where they do throughout the world.

The following chart lists the three sons of Noah, their sons, and several of the nations which came from their descendants.

THE DESCENDANTS OF NOAH AND THEIR NATIONS		
		–Gomer (Celts)
		–Magog (Scythians)
	JAPHETH (Aryan Race)	–Madai (Medes)
		–Javan (Greeks)
		–Tubal
		–Mesech
		–Tiras (Thracians)
NOAH	**HAM** (Turanian Race)	–Cush (Ethiopia)
		–Mizraim (Egypt)
		–Phut (Libya)
		–Canaan (Palestine)
		–Elam (Elamites)
	SHEM (Semitic Race)	–Asshur (Assyrians)
		–Arphaxad (Chaldeans)
		–Lud (Lydians)
		–Aram (Syrians)

The sons of Japheth settled in the area of the Black and Caspian Seas all the way west to Spain (Genesis 10:2–5). It is likely that the Greek and Germanic peoples descended from him.

History of the Human Race

Three of Ham's sons went into Africa (vs. 6–14). Later they spread northward to Shinar and Assyria. They built cities like Nineveh, Babel, and Accad (also spelled Akkad). Canaan, the fourth son of Ham, settled along the Mediterranean, extending from Sidon to Gerar near Gaza. The Canaanites used a language similar to the descendants of Shem although they were descendants of Ham.

The descendants of Shem occupied the area north of the Persian Gulf (vv. 21–31). They were also known as the Semites or the Semitic race. Elam, Asshur, and Aram are names associated with the Semites.

The following map shows the general area in which the descendants of Japheth, Ham, and Shem settled.

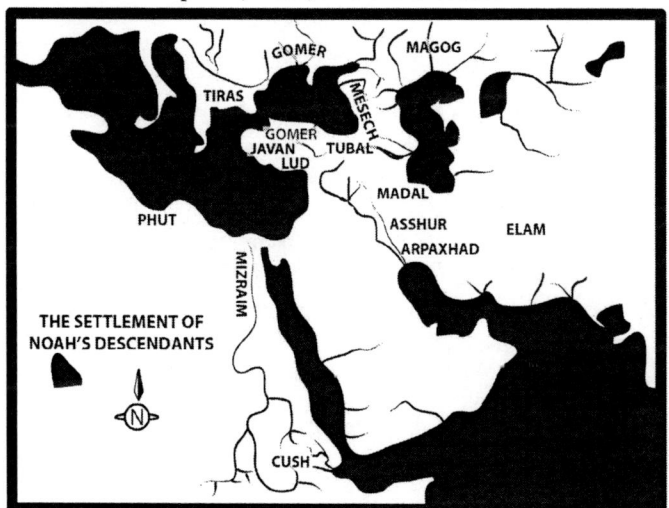

Application

16 What was God's ultimate reason for judging the world by the Flood?

. . . .

17 Review the chart, map, and descriptions of where the descendants of Noah settled. Then match each son with the places and nations that are associated with him and his descendants. Write the number of the son in front of each place (a–i) and nation (j–r) associated with him.

- ... **a** Accad
- ... **b** Africa
- ... **c** Aram
- ... **d** Asshur
- ... **e** Black Sea
- ... **f** Caspian Sea
- ... **g** Nineveh
- ... **h** Shinar
- ... **i** Spain

- ... **j** Assyrians
- ... **k** Celts
- ... **l** Chaldeans
- ... **m** Elamites
- ... **n** Ethiopia
- ... **o** Libya
- ... **p** Medes
- ... **q** Palestine
- ... **r** Scythians

1) Shem
2) Ham's sons
3) Japheth

Abraham and His Descendants

The Holy Spirit now narrows our attention to the Semites (Genesis 11:10–32). We are given a ten-generation account beginning with the family of Shem and ending with the family of Terah, who migrated from the city of Ur to Haran. It is to this family that Abram (later called Abraham) belonged. Abraham is an example of a man who acted on the revelation of creation as described in Psalm 19. God kept His promise to Abraham and led him by faith.

Abraham's seed or descendants—both natural and spiritual—occupy the center of interest throughout the rest of the Bible. They are called the people of God.

Application

18 Abraham is of special importance in a study of the Old Testament because his descendants
a) were very numerous.
b) were called the Levites.
c) are the people of God.

self-test

1 The account of Creation given in Genesis is important because it tells us
a) that God created the world from nothing.
b) the year when Creation took place.
c) where the Garden of Eden was located.

2 God wanted man to
a) be free from responsibility.
b) have dominion over creation.
c) love God because he had to.

3 Circle the letter of each TRUE statement below.
a) The Fall completely destroyed God's plans.
b) Satan told Eve the truth.
c) Only Adam and Eve were affected by the Fall.
d) An animal had to die so Adam and Eve could be covered.

4 The spiritual lesson illustrated by God's response to the offerings brought by Cain and Abel is that
a) God does not require offerings for sin.
b) there is no way for sin to be covered.
c) humans cannot cover sin by their own efforts.

5 Circle the letter in front of each statement which gives a correct description of the Fall.
a) Adam and Eve were created different from the animals. They sinned because they wanted to have authority over them. This made it necessary for them to leave the Garden.
b) Adam and Eve listened to Satan's suggestion to disobey God. Then they followed it, exercising their self-will to go against God's specific command.
c) Adam and Eve had enjoyed fellowship with God. But then they became more interested in caring for the Garden than in spending time in God's presence.

6 Noah was not destroyed by the Flood because he
a) was just and walked with God.
b) was the son of a righteous man.
c) had several godly children.

7 The descendants of Shem settled in the area
a) of the Black and Caspian Seas.
b) of north Africa.
c) north of the Persian gulf.

8 List the following events in the order in which they occurred. Write 1 before the one that happened first, 2 before the one that happened next, and so forth.

.... **a** Noah believed God's word and built the ark.

.... **b** Adam and Eve followed Satan's advice.

.... **c** Abel was murdered by his brother Cain.

.... **d** God created the heavens and the earth.

.... **e** Abraham was born.

.... **f** God sent the Flood in judgment upon sinful mankind.

.... **g** God gave man rulership and responsibility over creation.

.... **h** God made a covenant with humankind with the rainbow as a sign.

.... **i** Adam and Eve had to leave the Garden of Eden.

9 Circle the letter of each TRUE statement below.
a) Abraham belonged to the Semitic race.
b) Japheth was one of Abraham's ancestors.
c) Believers today belong to the people of God.

History of the Human Race

Answers To Study Questions

10 b) Mankind was subjected to physical death.
   c) Adam and Eve were exiled from the Garden.
   e) Adam and Eve were not allowed to eat of the tree of life.

1 a 3) World
  b 5) Human race
  c 6) Sin
  d 7) Redemption (Genesis 3:15 is regarded as a prophecy of Jesus Christ).
  e 1) Family
  f 4) Civilization
  g 2) Nations of the world

11 It teaches us that the only way sin can be covered is through death. Man's good efforts are not acceptable. (Your answer should be similar.)

2 a) False
  b) True
  c) True

12 b) was to be Christ's human ancestor.

3 b) God created the world by His word.

13 1) Adam
   2) Seth
   3) Enosh
   4) Kenan
   5) Mahalaleel
   6) Jared
   7) Enoch
   8) Methuselah
   9) Lamech
   10) Noah
   11) Shem

4 a) True
  b) False
  c) True

14 a) True
  b) False
  c) True

5 God's two main purposes for mankind were these:
  a) Mankind was to rule over creation, and
  b) mankind was to have fellowship with God. (Your answers should be similar but can be listed in any order.)

15 a) God promised that He would never again destroy the world with a flood.
  b) God's sign was the rainbow.

6 a) It was called the tree that gives knowledge of what is good and what is bad.
  b) God said that they were not to eat of its fruit.

16 God judged the world so that He could restore humankind's relationship with himself.

7 a 2
  b 1
  c 6
  d 3
  e 4
  f 5

17 a 2) Ham's sons
 b 2) Ham's sons
 c 1) Shem
 d 1) Shem
 e 3) Japheth
 f 3) Japheth
 g 2) Ham's sons
 h 2) Ham's sons
 i 3) Japheth
 j 2) Ham's sons
 k 3) Japheth
 l 1) Shem
 m 1) Shem
 n 2) Ham's sons
 o 2) Ham's sons
 p 3) Japheth
 q 2) Ham's sons
 r 3) Japheth

8 Here is the way I would answer this question:
 a) How good its fruit would be to eat.
 b) How beautiful the tree was.
 c) How wonderful it would be to become wise.
 (Your answers should be similar.)

18 c) are the people of God.

9 a) True
 b) False
 c) False

LESSON 3: History of the Chosen People

We have considered the origin of the world and the early history of humanity. Now our study turns to a single man and the beginning of a nation through whom God would bring about His purpose for humankind. That man was Abraham; it was from the twelve sons of his grandson, Jacob, that the nation of Israel descended.

God chose the Israelites to be His people because He wanted to have a people through whom He could accomplish His purposes in the world. His choice was intended to produce three important benefits. First, the worship of himself, the true God, would be preserved amid an increasing darkness coming upon the world. Second, His written Word, the Holy Scriptures, would be recorded, guarded, and passed on to future generations. And third, the line of ancestry for the needed and promised Redeemer, our Lord Jesus Christ, would be continued. The people of God who were to make these benefits possible were called to fulfill a great responsibility!

This lesson will help you see how God displayed His mighty power as He chose, preserved, and delivered His people. What wonderful miracles He did for them! You will gain new understanding of His purpose as you study these events.

History of the Chosen People

lesson outline

A Hope Is Given
A Man Responds
A Nation Is Born

lesson objectives

When you finish this lesson you should be able to:

- Show how the civilization described in Genesis 11 illustrates the pattern given in Romans 1.

- Describe God's calling of Abraham and His promises to him.

- Describe Abram's journey from Ur to Shechem.

- State how Abraham's faith was tested by each of his trials.

- Identify descriptions of Abraham's descendants and the relationship of each to the Israelites.

- Explain how the Israelites' experience in Egypt prepared them for what God wanted them to do next.

- Indicate the significance of the deliverance of the Israelites from Egypt.

learning activities

1. Read Genesis 11 through Exodus 14 in your Bible as the lesson directs you to.

2. Work carefully through the lesson development, answering the study questions and checking your answers with the ones that are given. Pay special attention to the teaching given concerning the life of Abraham. Take the self-test and check your answers.

key words

circumcision	patriarch
culture	plague
idols	providence
migrate	

lesson development

A HOPE IS GIVEN

The Darkness of the Times

Objective 1. *Show how the civilization described in Genesis 11 illustrates the pattern given in Romans 1.*

Read Genesis 11:1–9. The judgment of the Flood did not cause rebellion against God to stop. The people, who all spoke one language, made an evil and foolish plan. They built a city with a tower which was called the tower of Babel or Babylon. This tower seemed to be an effort to exalt themselves above the power of God himself, just like Satan had wanted to do (Luke 10:18, Isaiah 14:12–14). But God judged them. He confused their common language and scattered them over the earth, each group with a different language. Thus their ability for united rebellion was crushed. The rebellious condition of humankind described in Genesis 11 is a good example of the pattern given in Romans 1.

Application

1 Read Romans 1:19–29 and answer the following questions in your notebook.
a) What can be known about God through the things He has made (v. 20)?
b) How do people reject the truth of God (v. 21)?

First, the people reject the truth about God. Next, they follow five downward steps as they reject the truth.

1. Their empty minds are filled with darkness (v. 21).

2. They worship created images of men or animals (v. 23).

3. God gives them over to doing the filthy things they desire to do (v. 24).

4. God gives them over to following sexual perversions (vv. 26–27).

5. God gives them over to corrupted minds because they refuse to keep in mind the true knowledge about God (v. 28).

Therefore the corrupted condition of the people described in Genesis 11, like the corrupted condition described in Genesis 6, was the result of a human choice to reject the truth of God. Remember that all the people described in Genesis 11 were the direct descendants of Noah. They had the knowledge of God.

Historian Arnold Toynbee traced 21 separate civilizations in 6000 years of history. He began with the civilizations of Sumer and Akkad, which came into being soon after God judged the civilization described in Genesis 11. He ended with the recent civilizations of our world today. He found that each one has followed the same pattern of decline. The seed of rebellion which ultimately brings self-destruction is in all people.

Application

2 The civilization described in Genesis 11 is an illustration of the pattern given in Romans 1 because the people in it had
a) no godly ancestors who had followed God.
b) rejected the truth they once knew.
c) no knowledge or understanding of the truth.

The Faithfulness of God

Read Genesis 12:1–3

Objective 2. *Describe God's calling of Abram and His promises to him.*

The time period covered by Genesis 12–50 is known as the patriarchal age because it deals with the lives of the men who were known as the patriarchs—the physical (and spiritual) fathers of God's people. The patriarchs were Abram (later called Abraham) and his descendants Isaac, Jacob, and Joseph. Genesis 12–50 tells us about their relationships to God.

There are many wonderful truths we can learn from their lives. They struggled in their lives just as we do, yet they responded to God's revelation (His telling) and His guidance. We can be encouraged by studying their lives. Though they had human weaknesses and failings, they were sensitive to God's love. They believed in God's promise. They obeyed Him and experienced His presence in personal ways and were given a great hope for the future.

Abram's World

Abram (later called Abraham) was from the family of Terah, who lived in the city of Ur in Babylonia. Ur was located in the area called the fertile crescent, which we have already mentioned in Lesson 2. After the Flood, this area came to be ruled by the Sumerians, a non-Semitic people. But the Akkadians, a Semitic people, conquered them. The culture from which Abram came had probably existed in this area of the world for about 1,000 years. Notice these places on the following map.

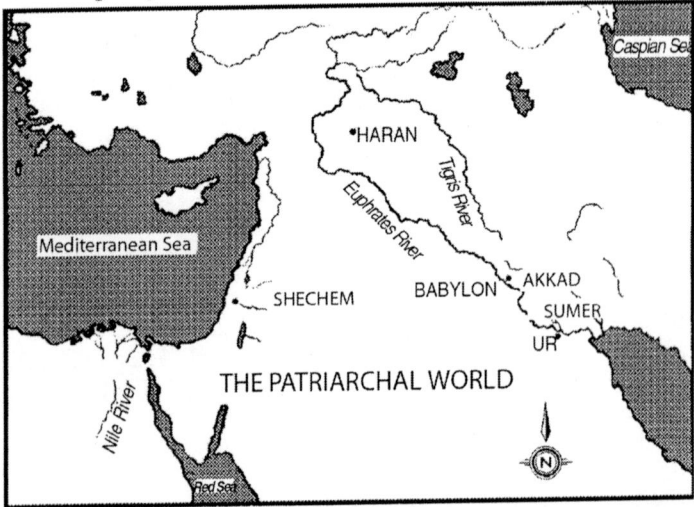

Ur was a thriving city with businesses, factories, courts, and religious activities. It covered more than 150 acres (60.7 hectares), and probably some 24,000 people lived there. Its idolatrous worship centered around a huge tower 70 feet (21.3 meters) tall.

Abram was a descendant of Noah through the line of Shem, as we have studied (Genesis 11:10–26). Yet Abram's father, Terah, and his people were far from any knowledge of the most high God. Terah and his family worshipped idols (Joshua 24:2–3).

Application

3 Review the description of Abram's world and study the foregoing map. Circle the letter of each TRUE statement below.
a) Ur is near the Caspian Sea.
b) The Sumerians were descendants of Shem, Noah's son.
c) Akkad is north of Sumer.
d) The Akkadians ruled after the Sumerians did.

God's Call and Promise

Though the times were dark and people worshipped idols, God was faithful! He continued to deal with humankind.

There must have been some testimony to truth in Abram's heart. Perhaps the message of creation, the first witness to God (Psalm 19), stirred him to search for God. We know that the call of God came to Abram even before his family migrated from Ur to Haran (Acts 7:2).

> The LORD had said to Abram, "Leave your country, your people and your father's household and go to the land I will show you. I will make you into a great nation and I will bless you; I will make your name great, and you will be a blessing. I will bless those who bless you, and whoever curses you I will curse; and all peoples on earth will be blessed through you." (Genesis 12:1–3)

Abram's experience from beginning to end was one of faith. The events which followed show the importance of one man's faith. First a family, then a tribe, then a nation, and finally the world were affected by Abram's faith in following God.

Application

4 Read Genesis 12:1–3 and write in your notebook answers to the following question.
a) What did God ask Abram to leave?
b) Where did God tell Abram to go?
c) What things did God promise Abram He would do?

A Man Responds

Abraham's Journey

Read Genesis 12:4–9

Objective 3. *Describe Abram's journey from Ur to Shechem.*

Abram responded to God's call for him to leave the security and prosperity of his native city of Ur. Hebrews 11:8 tells that "by faith Abraham, when called to go to a place he would later receive as his inheritance, obeyed and went, even though he did not know where he was going." But God had promised him a better place, and he eagerly looked and waited for it. He expected to find the city which was designed and built by God, the city with permanent foundations (Hebrews 11:10).

Abram first migrated about 600 miles (968 kilometers) north along a branch of the Euphrates river to Haran, a city very similar to Ur. Apparently he wavered in his resolution to do God's will, for he waited until Terah died before he fully obeyed the Lord. Then he left Haran and traveled 400 miles (645 kilometers) west and south into Canaan itself; to the place called Shechem.

According to Genesis 12:7–8 Abram twice built an altar. His activity was first of all a personal response in which he expressed his worship of the true God of heaven. It was also a witness to the idolatrous communities he lived in. He enjoyed such a close life with God that he received an unusual name.

Application

5 Read Isaiah 41:8 and James 2:23. Abram (later Abraham) was called God's
a) priest.
b) prophet.
c) friend.

6 Turn back to the preceding map and locate the places to which Abram migrated from Ur. Circle the letter in front of the statement which best describes his journey.
a) Abram left the city of Ur, then went 600 miles north to Haran and 400 miles southwest to Shechem.
b) Abram began his journey at the city of Ur, then went 1000 miles southwest along the Euphrates river to Shechem.
c) Abram left the city of Ur and ended his journey 600 miles north at the place called Shechem.

Abraham's Trials

Objective 4. *State how Abraham's faith was tested by each of his trials.*

The First Five Trials

Read Genesis 12:1–16:16. We will now study Abram's spiritual journey. It is more important for us to understand this journey than for us to know about the places where Abram traveled in his geographical journeys. In Nehemiah 9:7–8 a prophetic message was given to explain Abram's spiritual journey:

> "You are the LORD God, who chose Abram and brought him out of Ur of the Chaldeans and named him Abraham. You found his heart faithful to you, and you made a covenant with him to give to his descendants the land of the

Canaanites, Hittites, Amorites, Perizzites, Jebusites and Girgashites. You have kept your promise because you are righteous."

If we use this prophetic message as an outline of Abram's experience, we find that it describes four major events: 1) God chose Abram; 2) God changed Abram's name to Abraham; 3) God found that Abraham was faithful to Him; and 4) God made a covenant with Abraham and kept His promise. These four major events correspond with several different chapters in Genesis.

Abram's call is recorded in Genesis 12. In Genesis 15:7–21, God's covenant with Abram is described. Genesis 12–16 tells about an important time in Abram's relationship to God and reveals five specific tests by which God found that Abram was faithful to Him. The word found in the original language of the Bible means "thoroughly explore." Abram's faithfulness was brought to light; all of its aspects were made plain. Genesis 17 describes the event when Abram's name was changed to Abraham and God confirmed His covenant.

We will study the tests or trials of Abram in Genesis 12–16 in more detail because these relate to tests that we also may experience in our own lives. Carefully study the following chart and read the Scriptures given. The chart shows the five trials that Abram experienced before the covenant was confirmed.

Notice that the last of these tests involved delay. Twenty-four years had passed since Abram had settled in Canaan. Abram and Sarai had no hope for a son by any human means. Abram had considered appointing Eliezer, his servant from Damascus, as his heir (Genesis 15:2–4). Abram's suggestion probably shows that this was a custom of that time.

But God rejected Abram's idea. He had promised Abram and Sarai a son and said that through this son Abram's descendants would become as numerous as the stars of heaven. Abram believed God (Genesis 15:6), and this was the basis for God's acceptance of him. Romans 4:3 says that such faith is the basis of all righteousness with God.

Application

7 In the following chart, the last two columns have been left blank for you to fill in. The first three columns give the following information: a) the Scripture reference in which the trial is described, b) a short summary of the trial, and c) the context or circumstances of the trial. Issues refers to the aspects of the test that Abram had to overcome through faith and obedience. Reaction refers to the kinds of responses Abram made.

Read each of the Scriptures given in the references. Then in the two blank columns of the chart, write the issues relating to and the quality of faith tested by each trial. For issues, choose from these five ideas, matching them to the trials: riches, famine, separation, delay, and power. For reaction, choose from these five: fervent faith, humility, integrity, patience, and deficiency of faith.

THE TRIALS OF ABRAM (ABRAHAM)				
Scripture Reference	Description of Test	Context of Test	Issues	Reaction
1. Genesis 11–12	Willingness to break natural ties	Ur		
2. Genesis 12:10–20	Stress of circumstances (famine)	Egypt		
3. Genesis 13:1–18	Choice of unity or friction with Lot	Strife		
4. Genesis 14	Love for brothers and dependence on God	Kings of north and Sodom		
5. Genesis 16	Time of waiting for birth of son	His wife Sarai		

Other Events (Read Genesis 17:1–21:34; 23:1–20)

Abram's human weakness was shown again when he and Sarai planned that Hagar, Sarai's handmaid, should bear Abram a son. And through Hagar, Abram had a son who was named Ishmael. But in spite of Abram's error, God appeared to Abram again. He enlarged and confirmed the covenant He had made. Abram's name was changed to Abraham, Sarai's name was changed to Sarah, and God promised His blessing to all of Abraham's descendants including Ishmael (Genesis 17:1–18:15). The act of circumcision was made the sign or seal of the covenant. By receiving and giving circumcision, Abraham agreed to the covenant and acknowledged God's lordship of his life.

The destruction of Sodom and Gomorrah (Genesis 18–19), the incident of Abimelech (Genesis 20), the birth of Isaac, the child of promise (Genesis 21), and the death of Sarah (Genesis 23) are all events that take place during this time.

The Last Trial (Read Genesis 22:1–19)

For Abraham there was yet one more test of his relationship to God. It was the climactic and crucial one. Abraham had to move beyond his human reasoning to declare to Isaac that God himself would provide a lamb. Abraham's willingness to sacrifice his son demonstrated both his obedience and his ultimate faith in God. God the Father not only provided a ram for the sacrifice, but He also reaffirmed His promise to Abraham: "I will surely bless you and make your descendants as numerous as the stars in the sky and as the sand on the seashore. Your descendants will take possession of the cities of their enemies" (Genesis 22:17).

Application

8 Circle the letter of each TRUE statement below.
a) God asked Abraham to sacrifice Isaac.
b) Abraham told the servants that only he would return.
c) Abraham told Isaac that God would provide a lamb.
d) God was pleased with Abraham's obedience.

9 Which phrase best describes the qualities that were tested by Abraham's final trial?
a) Integrity and humility
b) Patience and waiting
c) Obedience and faith

10 Are you experiencing any circumstances through which your faith is being tested? In your notebook, describe these circumstances and the qualities of faith you must exercise in order to overcome them.

Abraham's Descendants

Objective 5. *Identify descriptions of Abraham's descendants and the relationship of each to the Israelites.*

We have studied Abraham's life in great detail because he personifies or represents the true issues of faith. Though we will not be able to deal as thoroughly with the lives of each of Abraham's descendants, we can learn many things about them.

The following diagram is a family tree, which shows the family relationships among the descendants of Abraham. The heavier lines show the parts of the family which the Bible tells about. The diagram indicates, for example, that Terah had three sons: Haran, Abraham, and Nahor. Below each of these sons, are the names of his descendants. However, some of these descendants married each other so they are connected by lines as well. Rebecca, the granddaughter of Nahor, married Isaac, the son of Abraham and Sarah. Rachel and Leah, the great-granddaughters of Nahor, married Jacob, the great-grandson of Abraham.

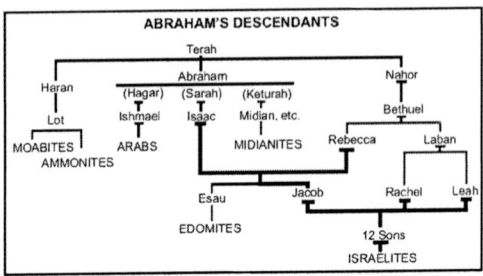

Application

11 Circle the letter in front of each of Abraham's descendants.
a) Rebecca
b) Lot
c) Arabs
d) Edomites
e) Jacob
f) Rachel
g) Israelites
h) Moabites

Do you remember the three purposes for which God chose a people? (See lesson introduction.) The third of these was to have a line of ancestry through which Jesus the Redeemer would come. Genesis 24–50 tells about three of Jesus' ancestors who were descendants of Abraham: Isaac, Jacob, and Joseph.

Isaac

Read Genesis 24:1–26:35. Isaac's story seems to be overshadowed by that of his father Abraham and his son Jacob. However, he was an important part of God's plan. Abraham saw to it that Isaac would not marry a Canaanite woman. Eliezer, Abraham's servant, followed Abraham's instructions and brought Isaac a wife from among Abraham's relatives in Mesopotamia (Genesis 24). God confirmed His covenant with Isaac (Genesis 26:5). Through Isaac, God's promises were passed on to his son Jacob.

Application

12 What division in Isaac's family is shown in Genesis 25:27–28?

....

....

Jacob

Read Genesis 27:1–37:1. Despite his failures, Jacob valued the covenant blessing of God. He seemed to be enthusiastic about God's promise of a nation that would bless the world. As we read his story, we see that he had to experience the consequences of his sin as all people do. God tested and chastised him, producing greatness in his life. He treated him as a son (see Hebrews 12:5–8).

Finally, Jacob's name, which meant deceiver, was changed to Israel, meaning a prince with God (Genesis 32:28). This was the name by which God's chosen people would be called—Israelites. Jacob's twelve sons were the heads of the twelve tribes which became the nation of Israel (Genesis 49).

Application

13 Both Isaac and Jacob made similar mistakes with their children. Read Genesis 37:3–4, and circle the letter in front of the sentence which describes this mistake.
a) Neither man showed his children much affection.
b) Both men showed special favor to one son.
c) Both men gave all their sons expensive gifts.

Joseph

Read Genesis 37:2–50:26. The account of Joseph is one of the fascinating stories in the Bible. It illustrates God's providence, which we can experience also. Joseph was sold as a slave into Egypt when he was 17. At 30 he became a ruler in Egypt. Ten years later, his father Jacob and the rest of the family entered Egypt during the time when there was a great famine in the entire fertile crescent. They numbered 70 persons. Because of Joseph, Pharaoh (the king of Egypt) permitted them to settle in Goshen, east of where the Nile river enters the Mediterranean Sea. This area was suitable for them to make their livelihood as shepherds. There they grew in number, wealth, and influence.

God had told Abraham that his descendants would spend many years as strangers in a foreign land (Genesis 15:13–16), so the book of Genesis appears to end in failure for God's people. The final idea is that of burial (Genesis 50:26). Yet God knew that the Israelites needed to develop in strength and increase in numbers so they would be able to possess the land of promise. They also must be kept from intermarriage with the Canaanites and from the influence of the Canaanites' idolatrous worship. During their time in Egypt, how wonderfully God built strength and purpose into His people!

Application

14 Review the preceding section. Then match the person's name (right side) to each phrase which describes him or her (left side).

... **a** He was the half-brother of Isaac.
... **b** He was also called "Israel."
... **c** Two of his descendants married Jacob.
... **d** He obtained the first-born rights of his brother.
... **e** She was the mother of Isaac.
... **f** She told Jacob to deceive his father.
... **g** God asked him to sacrifice his son.
... **h** The twelve tribes of Israel descended from his grandson Jacob.
... **i** He favored his son Esau.
... **j** He and his sons went to live in Egypt.
... **k** She favored her son Jacob.

1) Nahor
2) Abraham
3) Sarah
4) Isaac
5) Ishmael
6) Rebecca
7) Jacob

A Nation is Born

From a small group of 70 people who went to Egypt, the Israelites increased until they were an exceedingly large number. But in order to possess the land promised to the patriarchs, they needed to be delivered and prepared. They needed to be formed into a nation.

Although this preparation lasted only 40 years, it was so important that one-sixth of the Old Testament is devoted to describing it. This includes all of Exodus, Leviticus, Numbers, and most of Deuteronomy. A short outline of this description follows.

Egypt to Sinai	Exodus 1–18
Camp at Sinai	Exodus 19–Numbers 10:10
Wilderness Travel	Numbers 10:11–21
Camp at Moab	Numbers 22–Deuteronomy 34

Bondage and Slavery

Read Exodus 1–2

Objective 6. *Explain how the Israelites' experience in Egypt prepared them for what God wanted them to do next.*

As Genesis tells about the many failures of humanity, Exodus describes the powerful story of God hastening to rescue man. It is the great book of redemption—which means the buying back or buying out of slavery or captivity.

The name of the book itself means going out or way out. The opening chapters recount one of the most exciting and dramatic times in the history of God's people: how God gave them a way out, delivering them from the power of one of the mightiest rulers of their day—the Pharaoh of Egypt.

As Exodus begins, we read of the dark time when the hope God's people had for a promised land was at its lowest ebb. Joseph had died at 110 years of age, and a new king arose, "who did not know about Joseph" (Exodus 1:8). The Israelites, who had increased greatly in numbers and wealth, came under suspicion and were reduced to the most miserable slavery. It was a difficult time for them. Yet it led to the stirring of their almost-forgotten dreams—the promise of Canaan, the hope of being a special people of God.

It is indeed possible that the Israelites would never have left Egypt to go to the promised land if they had been comfortable and prosperous in Egypt. But God did not place their comfort as His highest interest. He wanted to develop their character and usefulness. God has a similar purpose for us—for we, too, are His people. We must keep this purpose constantly in mind.

Application

15 Review Exodus 1–2. The difficult experience the Israelites had in Egypt made them ready for what God wanted them to do next because they
a) became strong and numerous.
b) were comfortable and secure.
c) decreased and became weak.
d) cried out for help.

God's people had been strengthened and made hopeful through hardship. They were ready for the next steps in God's purpose to use them as a witness to himself.

Redemption and Deliverance

Objective 7. *Indicate the significance of the deliverance of the Israelites from Egypt.*

God Chooses a Man

Read Exodus 3–6. As we study God's plan for humanity, we see that it always involves a chosen man or woman. This was true when God brought the Israelites out of Egypt. During the last weary years of Israel's bondage, a son was born to parents in the tribe of Levi. Pharaoh had ordered that all males born to the Israelites were to be killed. But this son was hidden by his mother in a small basket which was left among the reeds in the Nile river.

The son was found by the daughter of the Pharaoh, who called him Moses, a word meaning to draw out, for she had drawn him out of the water. Through the influence of Moses' older sister, Moses' own mother was brought to care for him. The events of Moses' life lead us to conclude that his mother taught him things about his people and the living God.

After his early years which he spent under his mother's care, Moses was raised in the court of the king and had the wealth of Egypt at his command. He learned many things during the 40 years in Pharaoh's palace. Yet, he did not cease to identify with his people the Israelites, even in wrong ways (Exodus 2:11–16). Moses was imperfect like all of us are. God had to put him into the desert of Midian for the second major part of his education, where he lived for the next 40 years of his life.

Finally, when Moses was 80 years old, the eternal God appeared to him. As Moses stood at the burning bush in the desert of Midian, God said to him,"'I am the God of your father, the God of Abraham, the God of Isaac, and the God of Jacob'" (Exodus 3:6). This affirmation linked Him with the covenant promises made to the patriarchs. God told Moses what things His plan for Moses' life included (Exodus 3:1–4:17). During the last 40 years of his life, Moses led God's people out of Egypt and toward the promised land.

Application

16 Moses is referred to many times in the Bible. Review Exodus 1–3 and read Acts 7:22–30. Match the place (right side) to each description of what Moses learned there (left side).

... **a** To know God

... **b** That he was an Israelite

... **c** That God would send him to Pharaoh

... **d** The wisdom of Egypt

1) His mother's home
2) In Pharaoh's palace
3) In the desert of Midian

17 According to Hebrews 11:24, Moses made several important choices. Match the choice (right side) with each description of what it involved (left side).

... **a** have the treasures of Egypt

... **b** keep his eyes on the future reward.

... **c** be called the son of the king's daughter.

... **d** suffer with God's people.

... **e** enjoy sin for a little while.

1) Moses chose to
2) Moses refused to

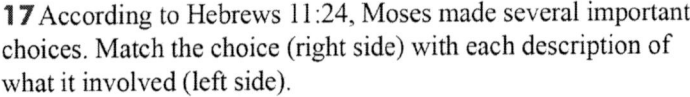

It was Moses who wrote the Pentateuch (the first five books of the Bible). His training in Egypt along with his spiritual experience would have given him the necessary ability to do this important task.

God Delivers the Israelites

Read Exodus 7–14. Freeing God's people from a Pharaoh of overwhelming power looked like an impossible task. The might of Egypt had greatly increased; it extended from Egypt through Palestine up to the Euphrates area.

When Moses later asked Pharaoh to release God's people, Pharaoh replied, "'Who is the Lord, that I should obey him and let Israel go?'" (Exodus 5:2). God supported Moses' request with supernatural plagues. The first nine plagues were similar to natural events that sometimes happened in the Nile River valley—dead fish, swarms of dying frogs, lice and gnats, swarming insects and pestilence, boils and crop-destroying hail. The last one was a judgment on all of the gods of Egypt.

At first Pharaoh remained stubborn, or as the Hebrew language says it, he hardened his heart. Then God made him stubborn, or as the Hebrew language says, caused his heart to stand firm. Thus we see that God only made more sure what Pharaoh himself had already decided. Pharaoh by his own will made the decision to resist, but God held him to it for His own glory. The plagues demonstrated the power of Israel's God to both the Egyptians and the Israelites. Each plague brought greater realization of God's supernatural power. Finally, God sent the last plague. The results of this one were so severe that the Egyptians insisted that the Israelites leave immediately (Exodus 12:33).

Application

18 Review Exodus 12:21–36 and answer the following questions in your notebook.
a) What did Moses tell the Israelites to do (vv. 21–22)?
b) What did Moses say God would do (v. 23)?
c) What happened to the Egyptians (v. 29)?
d) What two things did the Egyptians do (vv. 31, 35–36)?
e) Why was this event called the Passover?

The Israelites left at once, carrying with them the wealth of Egypt. They went towards the Red Sea. This was not the most direct way to Canaan. By the well-traveled coastal road, which was used for commercial and military purposes, they could have reached Canaan in two weeks. But God chose to lead them towards the Red Sea. Remember, they were a disorganized mass of former slaves. Time and opportunity for them to become united was very important. God did not want them to turn back to Egypt. And He was going to do one more mighty act. This act would have a great effect on the Egyptians; they would know that He was the Lord (Exodus 14:4).

God led the people by a pillar of cloud in the day and a pillar of fire by night. He himself was there. When the Egyptians changed their minds and came out against the Israelites, God moved the cloud of glory behind His people, between them and their enemies. God used a strong east wind to open a way through the sea, and the Israelites crossed over. They watched as the Egyptian army was covered by the sea while trying to follow them. God had delivered His people!

Application

19 What effect did this miracle have on the Israelites (Exodus 14:31)?

....

20 Circle the letter of each TRUE statement.
a) God caused Pharaoh to decide to resist Him.
b) The firstborn sons of the Israelites were spared because the Israelites lived in Goshen.
c) Pharaoh asked the Israelites to leave.
d) The Israelites did not go directly to Canaan.

21 God miraculously delivered His people. This deliverance was significant because it showed that
a) Moses convinced Pharaoh to change his mind.
b) the Israelites were clever and wise.
c) there was no god like the Lord.
d) the Israelites were a great nation.

There was much ahead for the Israelites to learn. There was discipline and chastisement. There were miraculous provisions and lessons of leadership. But a nation was born in a day, born on the basis of blood being shed. This was the nation and people of God.

History of the Chosen People

self-test

1 In what way did the civilization described in Genesis 11 illustrate the pattern given in Romans 1?
a) They had rejected God's truth and were rebellious.
b) They had no knowledge of God at all.
c) They began to worship images made like reptiles.

2 God's call to Abram was to
a) have many descendants.
b) become a great nation.
c) leave his native land.

3 Circle the letter of the phrase which gives the places of Abram's journey in the correct order.
a) Haran, Ur, Shechem
b) Shechem, Ur, Haran
c) Ur, Haran, Shechem

4 Abraham's reaction to his last and crucial trial was that of
a) humility.
b) obedience.
c) patience.

5 The twelve tribes of Israel descended from the twelve sons of
a) Abraham.
b) Jacob.
c) Joseph.

6 Circle the letter in front of each TRUE statement.
a) Abram's (Abraham's) faith was tested after God had promised him many descendants.
b) Abraham received the sign of circumcision after he had already believed in God's word.
c) Jacob entered Egypt before Joseph did.
d) The man whose name meant deceiver received a new name meaning a prince with God.
e) Pharaoh's palace was the place where Moses came to know God.
f) When the Israelites left Egypt they were ready to enter the promised land.

answers to study questions

11 c) Arabs
d) Edomites
e) Jacob.
g) Israelites

1 a) His eternal power and His divine nature can be known.
b) They refuse to honor God or give Him thanks.

12 Isaac favored Esau and Rebecca favored Jacob; this caused Jacob and Esau to be divided from one another.

2 b) rejected the truth they once knew.

13 b) Both men showed special favor to one son.

3 a) False
b) False
c) True
d) True

14 a 5) Ishmael
b 7) Jacob
c 1) Nahor
d 7) Jacob
e 3) Sarah
f 6) Rebecca
g 2) Abraham
h 2) Abraham
i 4) Isaac
j 7) Jacob
k 6) Rebecca

4 a) He asked him to leave his native land, his relatives, and his father's house.
b) He told him to go to a country that God would show him.
c) He promised to give him many descendants, make his name famous, and bless the whole world through him. (Your answers should be similar.)

History of the Chosen People **79**

15 a) became strong and numerous.
  d) cried out for help.

 5 c) friend.

16 a 3) In the desert of Midian.
  b 1) His mother's home.
  c 3) In the desert of Midian.
  d 2) In Pharaoh's palace.

 6 a) Abram left the city of Ur, then went 600 miles north to Haran and 400 miles southwest to Shechem.

17 a 2) Moses refused to
  b 1) Moses chose to
  c 2) Moses refused to
  d 1) Moses chose to
  e 2) Moses refused to

 7 No. 1: ....
Separation; Fervor of Faith.
  No. 2: Famine; Sufficiency of Faith.
  No. 3: Riches; Humility.
  No. 4: Power; Integrity.
  No. 5: Delay; Patience.

18 a) He told each family to kill a lamb or goat and put its blood on the door posts and beam of their house. They were to stay inside all night.
  b) He would see the blood and would not slay their firstborn.
  c) All their firstborn sons were slain.
  d) They told the Israelites to leave, and they gave them jewelry and clothes.
  e) Because the Lord passed over the homes of Israel and spared their firstborn sons.

 8 a) True
  b) False
  c) True
  d) True

19 They had deep respect and awe towards the Lord and put faith in Him and His servant Moses. (Your answer should be similar.)

9 c) Obedience and faith

20 a) False
   b) False
   c) True
   d) True

10 Your answer. Perhaps you are facing some of the issues Abraham did. You can be victorious just as he was.

21 c) there was no god like the Lord.

For Your Notes

LESSON 4: History of Faith and Worship

Now, with their years of slavery behind them, the people of God needed to be trained. Such a process would take time. The location of God's "school" for His people was the desert, and the time they spent there was to be one of rich religious experience and education. Laws were to be given, learned, and put into practice. The hearts of the people were to be knit to their leaders and to each other. The Israelites must be made to understand their mission. And the life of the desert was needed to produce a people hardy and sturdy enough to be God's sword against the Canaanites.

As you study this lesson you will follow the Israelites as they journeyed toward the promised land. You will see them as they progressed and were delayed. You will learn about the various means God used to bring order and unity among them. You will discover, too, the spiritual truths that are pictured by the particular objects and observances that God chose.

Your understanding of what faith and worship involves will be greatly enriched through the material in this lesson. You will also see how God's people were prepared through their experiences to possess the land He had promised them.

lesson outline

God's People Are Prepared
God's People Doubt and Wander
God's People Hear Final Instructions

lesson objectives

When you finish this lesson you should be able to:

- Describe places and events in Israel's journey from the Red Sea to Sinai.

- Indicate the meaning and purpose of the Law for Israel and all believers.

- Explain the spiritual significance of the tabernacle furniture.

- Describe ways in which the priesthood illustrated the way believers should serve God.

- Match the names of the offerings to their meanings.

- Discuss how the special seasons related to people's experiences and relationship to God.

- State the spiritual principle illustrated by the organization of the camp of Israel.

- Describe Israel's doubt and wandering and the spiritual lessons these events teach.

- Summarize the final instructions given by Moses in the book of Deuteronomy.

learning activities

1. Read from your Bible as directed. It is important for you to fulfill the reading assignments so that you will become acquainted with the content of each Old Testament book. (Lessons 4–10 cover the major themes of these readings but not all the details you will find as you read.)

2. Complete the lesson.

3. Reviewed Unit 1 (Lessons 1–4), complete Unit Student Report 1 and return Answer Sheet 1 to your national GU office if you live outside the United States or to your local church's CED learning center coordinator if you live in the United States.

(If you are currently incarcerated in a jail or prison in the United States you may mark your answers on the scantron answer sheet provided and send to the following address: CED, Global University, 1211 S. Glenstone Ave., Springfield, MO 65804.)

key words

ceremonial law	legalism	peninsula
civil law	manna	priest
consecration	Messiah	veil
Decalogue	moral law	
feast	offering	

History of Faith and Worship 85

lesson development

GOD'S PEOPLE ARE PREPARED

Objective 1. *Describe places and events in Israel's journey from the Red Sea to Sinai.*

For Israel their exodus, or way out from Egypt was one of the greatest events in their experience. The following map shows the route they traveled, which is represented by a broken line. As you read about their journey, find on this map each place that is mentioned. (Read Exodus 15–19.)

After the Israelites left Egypt, their journey to Canaan by way of the Sinai peninsula was by God's divine order. (The Sinai peninsula is the land between the Red Sea on the west and the Gulf of Aquaba on the east.)

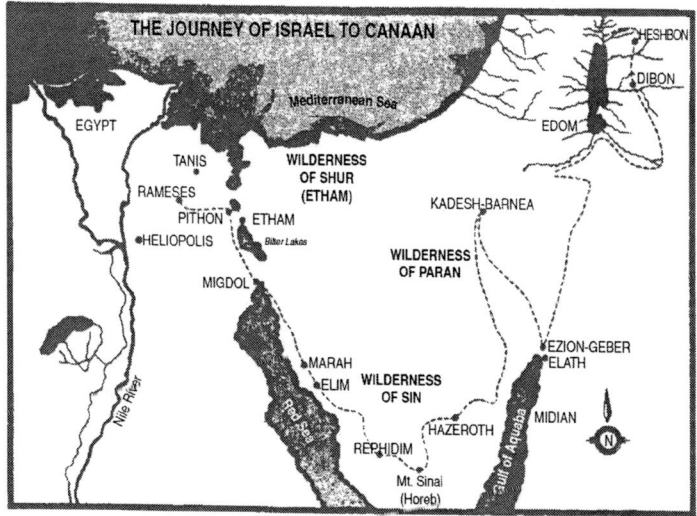

After God defeated the Egyptians by His mighty power, there came a time of triumphant praise (Exodus 15). This was followed by a three-day journey into the wilderness of Shur. At Maran, the bitter waters were made sweet by a miracle (Exodus 15:25). The Israelites then went south, camping at Elim.

In the wilderness of Sin, God miraculously provided manna. Manna meant *what is this?* in the language of the people. It was a mysterious, good-to-eat, and concentrated food which was to be Israel's daily food until they entered Canaan. Quails were supplied in abundance when the Israelites craved meat like they had eaten in Egypt.

At Rephidim, three significant things happened: 1) God provided a gushing torrent of water when Moses struck the rock with his rod; 2) Amalek was turned back by the Israelite army under Joshua while Moses prayed; and 3) Moses followed his father-in-law's advice and appointed elders to help him carry out his overwhelming duties.

In less than three months the Israelites arrived at Mount Sinai (also called Horeb). They were to camp there for almost one year. There they were to learn their destiny and purpose under God.

Application

1 Circle the letter of each TRUE statement below.
a) It took the Israelites about 12 weeks to arrive at Sinai.
b) At Elim, the bitter waters were made sweet.
c) The wilderness of Shur is south of the Sinai peninsula.
d) Mt. Sinai is located west of the Gulf of Aquaba.

God's Law and Its Purpose

Objective 2. *Indicate the meaning and purpose of the Law for Israel and all believers.*

One year of living in a camp around Mt. Sinai was sufficient for God's covenant people to become a nation. First, the Decalogue (which means the ten laws or commandments) was given to them. Then the specific laws for holy living were given. A place for God to dwell among the people and for their worship of Him was constructed. This place was called the tabernacle or the tent of the Lord's presence. In addition, the priesthood was organized, the offerings put in order, and the feasts and seasons begun. In short, Israel was being made ready to serve God effectively.

For centuries, the Israelites had known that their fathers—Abraham, Isaac, and Jacob—had enjoyed a covenant with God. Now that same God was revealing himself to them. His power was no longer something that others had felt, it became an experience in their own lives. They saw His miracles for themselves!

At Sinai, Israel prepared for three days for the covenant to be established. God revealed to Moses the Decalogue, the other laws, and the directions for the sacred feasts. God spoke to the people in the midst of fire and cloud. Aaron, two of his sons, and seventy elders led the people in making the burnt offerings. After Moses read the book of the covenant, the people responded by accepting the law. Then the covenant was sealed with the blood of the sacrifices. The condition of the covenant was obedience. Under the covenant, members of the nation could give up their rights by disobedience.

The laws God gave can be divided into three types:

1. Moral Law—Rules of Right and Wrong

2. Civil Law—Rules for the Nation

3. Ceremonial Law—Rules of Worship

The moral law was permanent. But many of the civil and ceremonial laws were given for a limited period of time. For example, certain laws concerning the killing of animals were changed when Israel entered Canaan (compare Leviticus 17 to Deuteronomy 12:20–24).

Application

2 Read Exodus 24:1–8. Why do you think that the covenant was sealed with the blood of a sacrifice?

. . . .

The Moral Law (Read Exodus 20:1–26)

The moral law is made up of the Decalogue or ten commandments. These were first spoken by God, and then they were written down. Following is a short version of these ten important laws, which are first found in Exodus 20:3–17.

1. Worship no god but Me.
2. Do not make for yourselves images of anything.
3. Do not use My name for evil purposes.
4. Observe the Sabbath and keep it holy.
5. Respect your father and your mother.
6. Do not commit murder.
7. Do not commit adultery.
8. Do not steal.
9. Do not accuse anyone falsely.
10. Do not desire what belongs to another man.

The first two laws are the ones that show the special nature of the Decalogue. They forbid the worship of idols or any other gods. Egypt, from which Israel had come, worshipped many gods. Canaan, to which Israel was marching, was also filled with idolatry. God's people had to be different! They must express devotion only to the true God.

After these commandments had been given to Israel, however, the people sinned. While Moses was in the holy mountain they made a golden idol shaped like a bull and worshipped it (Exodus 32:1–10). In Egypt the Israelites probably had joined the Egyptians in their worship of the god Apis, who was represented by an image of a bull. Now at Sinai, the Israelites themselves made and worshipped the same kind of image. This showed that they had not really turned away from worshipping other gods as the Decalogue commanded. Their action demonstrated the great need for total separation from heathen practices as the Law required.

Application

3 Read the ten commandments. Write the number of each group (right side) in front of the subject it deals with (left side).

- ... **a** Relationship to family
- ... **b** Relationship to other people
- ... **c** Relationship to God
- ... **d** Relationship to other people's property

1) Laws 1–4
2) Law 5
3) Laws 6, 7, 9
4) Laws 8, 10

The moral law shows how humans must live in order to be accepted by God. But no person can keep it perfectly, so it shows up humanity's sinfulness. The purpose of the entire moral law is the same today as it was for the Israelites. The New Testament teaches us that the law shows a) God's holiness, b) humanity's sinfulness, and c) our need for God's righteousness (Romans 3:19–31).

During Old Testament times, God required men to offer sacrifices. These sacrifices temporarily covered people's sins and failures to keep the Law. The Law itself had no provision for failure. Since it was given, only one man has been able to keep it perfectly, and that man was Jesus Christ, God's Son. Christ not only kept the Law but also paid the complete penalty for the broken Law. That penalty was death. He died that we might live. He was the perfect sacrifice (Hebrews 9:13–15; 10:1–22, 1 Peter 1:18–20).

Abraham is an Old Testament example of how God puts people right with himself. God accepted Abraham 13 years before Abraham was circumcised (Genesis 15:6) and 430 years before the Law was added to show what sin was (Galatians 3:15–18). It was impossible, then, for Abraham to have been accepted because he had kept the Law. It is important to understand this! It will help us to avoid thinking that believers today must keep all the Old Testament laws in order to be accepted by God.

Paul wrote, "Now a righteousness from God, apart from law, has been made known, to which the Law and the Prophets testify" (Romans 3:21). But God now puts people right with himself on the basis of Christ's sacrifice and their faith in Him (Romans 3:22–26). Thus we may make a contrast between Mt. Sinai with its horror, thunder, and lightning (Exodus 19) and Mt. Calvary where a meeting place between God and the sinner is made possible by the blood of Jesus Christ. The following diagram illustrates these points.

THE LAW OF THE PROMISE OF GOD

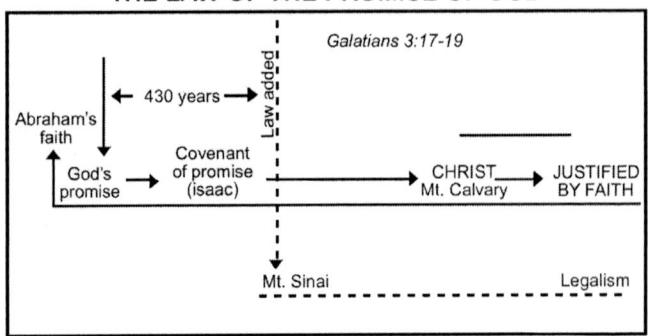

So God's eternal plan, as we have seen, is to declare us righteous by our faith and trust in Him. That is always the basic covenant of His kingdom. Our righteousness can never come by way of the Law. But the Law still has its purposes. It shows us our need for a savior. It also represents God's standard for living. Jesus summed up the spirit of the Law in Matthew 22:34–40. He said that we should love God with all our heart and love our neighbor as ourselves.

Application

4 Write the short form of each of the ten commandments in your notebook. Then after each one list one or two ways in which you can apply it to your life.

Civil Law (Read Exodus 21:1–23:9; Leviticus 18)

God gave His people laws which related to every area of living; these laws are known as the civil law. His people were not to follow the evil ways of the Egyptians and the Canaanites. Laws about motherhood and childbirth were necessary because of sexual perversion, prostitution, and child sacrifice, which were common among the Canaanites. Laws forbidding brother and sister marriages were also given because these were common in Egypt. The more a person knows about the cultures of Egypt and Canaan the easier it is to understand the Law's restrictions!

Ceremonial Law

The ceremonial law, or the rules of worship, includes laws relating to the tabernacle, the priesthood, the feasts, the offerings, and the organization of the camp. It is described in the following section.

Application

5 Circle the letter of the statement that best describes the purpose of the Law.
a) The Law gives us God's rules to follow so we can become righteous by obeying them.
b) The Law makes us realize our sinful condition and shows us we need God's righteousness.

God's Organization and Its Purpose

Every country celebrates some day in which its citizens recognize their national existence or freedom. From Mt. Sinai on, the Israelites celebrated their existence as a special people for God's use. But emotion and sentiment are not enough! God organized His people so that they might walk in their commitment. This organization, described in the ceremonial laws, took five basic forms. For the believer, each of them is like a rich vein in a gold mine. They singly and together point to the true kingdom of God. Each gives us an illustration (called a figure or type) of Jesus, God's chosen one or Messiah, or pictures Him in some way. These forms had to do with five basic areas of Israel's spiritual life. Also, they illustrate truths which apply in a similar manner to the lives of believers today. These five forms are as follows:

Form of Organization	Illustration
1. The tent of the Lord's presence and its furnishings	1. God living among humans and giving them a way to come to Him
2. The priesthood	2. The ways in which people serve God
3. The offerings	3. The means by which people worship God
4. The feasts or seasons	4. The ordering of a person's life and experience in God
5. The numbering and organzing of tribes	5. Spiritual warfare

If you were to write a study of even one of these applications, you would need a whole book. This course can give only the main points of the truths they teach. Perhaps the Holy Spirit will inspire you to study them in greater detail on your own!

Application

6 The form which had to do with spiritual warfare was the
a) tabernacle (tent of the Lord's presence).
b) numbering and organization of the tribes.
c) priesthood.

The Tent of the Lord's Presence
(Read Exodus 23–27; 30–40)

Objective 3. *Explain the spiritual significance of tabernacle furniture.*

The tent of the Lord's presence, also called the tabernacle, is emphasized in many chapters of the Bible. For example, more than one-third of the verses in the book of Hebrews refer to the tabernacle.

The tabernacle was built to provide a way for God to have fellowship with His people; He wanted to live among them (Exodus 25:8). God gave Bezalel of the tribe of Judah and Oholiab of the tribe of Dan special ability to do the work.

In building the tabernacle, the people of God were invited to make freewill or voluntary contributions. The men brought gold and silver. They cut down acacia trees and brought them; these were desert trees supported by deep tap-roots into underground streams. Their wood was practically indestructible! The women brought the finest of their spun and woven cloth. According to Genesis 15:14 and Exodus 12:35–36, the Israelites had carried away the wealth of the Egyptians with them. This was where they got the precious materials used to build the tabernacle. In this way a portable structure of rare fineness was made. For hundreds of years it continued to be a place where God's people gathered and worshipped.

Application

7 Why do you think God had the tabernacle made so that it was portable?

. . . .

Refer to the following diagram as you study the various parts of the tabernacle and its furnishings.

THE TABERNACLE AND ENCLOSURE

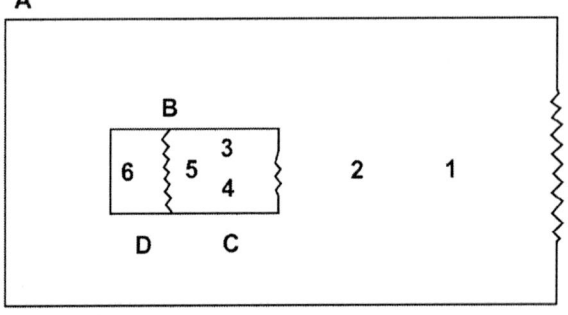

The tabernacle was set in the midst of a court which was enclosed by 450 feet (137 meters) of fine linen curtains (**A**). These were hung on bronze pillars spaced 7½ feet (2.3 meters) apart. The only entrance was at the east end; it was 30 feet (9 meters) wide (Exodus 27:9–18; 38:9–20).

When the Israelite entered, he made his offering in the open area at the altar of sacrifice (**1**). This altar was covered with bronze and was portable, like the other furnishings (Exodus 27:1–8; 38:1–7). A bronze basin where the priests had to cleanse themselves (**2**) also stood in this court (Exodus 30:17–21; 38:8; 40:30). This court, furnished mostly with bronze, stands for judgment upon sin. The offerings made there were consumed or tested by fire.

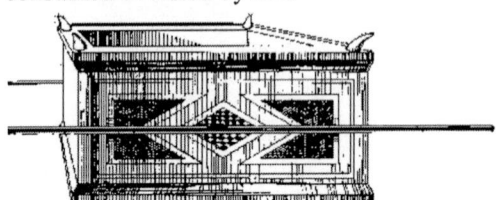

ALTAR OF SACRIFICE (1)

BRONZE BASIN (2)

In the western half of the court was the tabernacle itself (**B**). Its length was 45 feet (13.7 meters) and its width was 15 feet (4.6 meters). It was divided into two parts: the Holy Place (**C**) and the Holy of Holies or Most Holy Place (**D**). The Holy Place measured 30 feet by 15 feet (9.1 meters by 4.6 meters) and the Most Holy Place measured 15 feet by 15 feet (4.6 meters by 4.6 meters). There was only one entrance, which opened from the east into the Holy Place. Only priests could go in. Beyond a veil was the Most Holy Place. Into this part only the high priest could enter, and only on one day a year—the day of covering or atonement.

Against the north side of the Holy Place stood the table of bread (**3**). On the south side the lampstand was placed (**4**). In front of the veil which divided the Most Holy Place from the Holy Place was located the altar of incense (**5**). All of these furnishings were covered with gold.

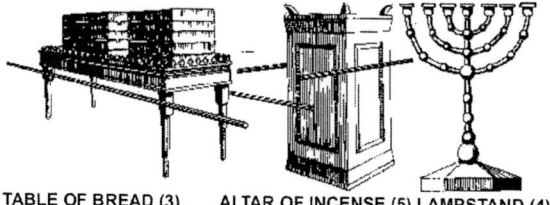

TABLE OF BREAD (3)   ALTAR OF INCENSE (5) LAMPSTAND (4)

The Most Holy Place contained the most sacred object in the religion of Israel. It was called the ark of the Lord or the ark of the covenant (**6**). It was made of acacia wood and overlaid inside and outside with pure gold. It was 3 feet 9 inches long (1.1 meters) and had a depth and width of 2 feet 9 inches (84 centimeters) according to Exodus 25:10–22 and 37:1–9. The cover of the box or chest was called the mercy seat.

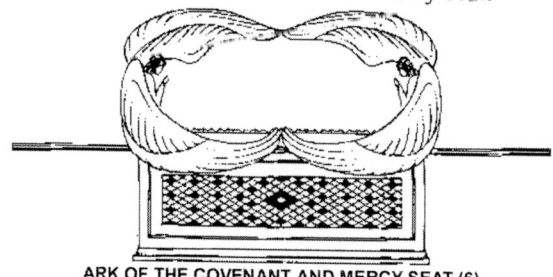

ARK OF THE COVENANT AND MERCY SEAT (6)

Two winged creatures made of gold overshadowed the center of the mercy seat, which represented God's presence. Unlike the other nations, who represented their gods with idols, no object was used to represent the God of Israel. Nevertheless, the mercy seat was the place where God and man met (Exodus 30:6), and where God spoke to man (Exodus 25:22, Numbers 7:89). It was the place where on the Day of Atonement the high priest sprinkled the blood for the sins of the nation of Israel (Leviticus 16:14).

The stone tablets on which the Decalogue was written were placed inside the ark (Exodus 25:21; 31:18, Deuteronomy 10:3–5). Later on, a pot of manna and Aaron's rod were also put into the ark (Exodus 16:32–34, Numbers 17:1–11).

The construction and furnishings of the tabernacle picture aspects of Christ and His work. For example, each of the seven pieces of furniture (counting the mercy seat as a separate piece) represents a specific spiritual truth.

Application

8 On the diagram of the tabernacle, write the name of each article of furniture beside the number showing where it was located.

9 Match each article or furnishing (right side) with the spiritual truth you think it best represents (left side).

... **a** Praise and prayer and the fragrance of Christ's perfect life

... **b** God dwelling among His people

... **c** The cross of Christ and judgment upon sin

... **d** Communion with Jesus, the bread of life

... **e** Cleansing and forgiveness of sin

... **f** Mercy given because of shed blood

... **g** Christ, the light of the world

1) Altar of sacrifice
2) Bronze basin
3) Table of bread
4) Lampstand
5) Altar of incense
6) Ark of the Covenant
7) Mercy seat

Of course these are only some of the spiritual meanings these objects can represent. There are many others as well.

The Priesthood (Read Exodus 28–29; Leviticus 8–10)

Objective 4. *Describe ways in which the priesthood illustrated the way believers should serve God.*

God's purpose that Israel be a holy nation demanded an orderly worship. God therefore chose Aaron, Moses' brother, to serve as high priest. Aaron's four sons, Nadab, Abihu, Eleazar, and Ithamar were to help him.

Before this official priesthood was begun, the head of each house (the patriarch) represented his family in the worship of God. Only one priest is mentioned earlier in Scripture. He was the mysterious Melchizedek in Genesis 14:18. Since the Passover in Egypt, the first-born son of every Israelite family belonged to God (Exodus 13:1–2). The people's sin in making the golden bull caused God to choose the Levites (male members of the tribe of Levi) as substitutes for the oldest son of each family (Numbers 3:5–13; 8:17).

The priests offered sacrifices and led the people in making atonement for sin (Exodus 28:1–43, Leviticus 16:1–34). They helped discern the will of God for the people (Numbers 27:21, Deuteronomy 33:8). They were responsible for caring for and supervising the tabernacle with the help of the Levites. As guardians of the Law, they were also the teachers of the nation.

The priests were required to live holy (Leviticus 21:1–22:10). There were special clothes for them (Exodus 28:40–43; 39:27–29) and for the high priest also (Exodus 28:4–39). The priests and the high priest went through a ceremony of consecration (Exodus 29:1–37; 40:12–15; Leviticus 8:1–36). All of these matters are worthy of further study when you have opportunity. Now, however, we will consider how they relate to our lives as Christians.

We are called to serve God also. First Peter 2:5–9 tells us that believers today are like the priests of Old Testament times in some ways. Like those priests, believers should also live lives that are separated from the world. Much can be learned from the Old Testament priesthood about what it means to serve God.

Application

10 Compare 1 Peter 2:5–9 to the passages of Scripture on the priesthood given in the preceding section. In your notebook, write two ways in which the priesthood illustrated how believers should serve God today.

The Offerings (Read Leviticus 1–7)

Objective 5. *Match the names of the offerings to their meanings.*

The practice of making offerings to God did not begin at Mt. Sinai. Sacrifices and offerings to God had undoubtedly been a regular procedure. The records concerning Cain, Abel, and Noah indicate this. Remember that Moses spoke of such offerings to Pharaoh (Exodus 5:1–3, 18:12, and 24:5). But the sacrificial laws given at Mt. Sinai were meant to provide specific instructions for such worship.

There were offerings of five kinds. In four of these, blood was shed: 1) the sin offering, 2) the trespass offering, 3) the burnt offering, and 4) the peace offering. In the fifth kind, the meal offering, no blood was shed. For the first four offerings, acceptable animals were those that were clean and tame such as sheep, goats, or oxen. Israelites who were extremely poor were allowed to substitute pigeons.

The general procedure for making each offering where blood was shed was this:

1. The Israelite presented the animal at the altar.

2. He then placed his hand on the animal, testifying that it was offered in substitution for him.

3. The animal was slain.

4. The blood was sprinkled, generally at the base of the altar.

History of Faith and Worship

5. The sacrifice was burned in whole or in part depending upon the offering.

These offerings and sacrifices were related to human needs and behaviors. In the chart below, notice the purpose each one had and read the Bible verses that describe the offering.

Offering	Purpose	Bible References
Sin	To deal with sins done in ignorance	Leviticus 4:1–35; 6:24–30
Trespass	To deal with the neglect of the rights of a person or of God	Leviticus 5:14–6:7; 7:1–7
Burnt	To express consecration	Leviticus 1:3–17; 6:8–13
Peace (Fellowship)	To express thanksgiving, a vow, or a freewill sacrifice; it represented fellowship between God and man	Leviticus 3:1–17; 7:11–34; 19:5–8; 22:21–25
Meal (or Grain)	Represented the fruit of man's labor and stood for service offered to God.	Leviticus 2:1–16; 6:14–23

Carefully study the following diagram. Notice that the order in which God gave the offerings in Leviticus started with the peace (communion), meal (service), and burnt (surrender) offerings—all voluntary. In contrast, the order in which man came to God began with the sin and trespass offerings—both compulsory or required.

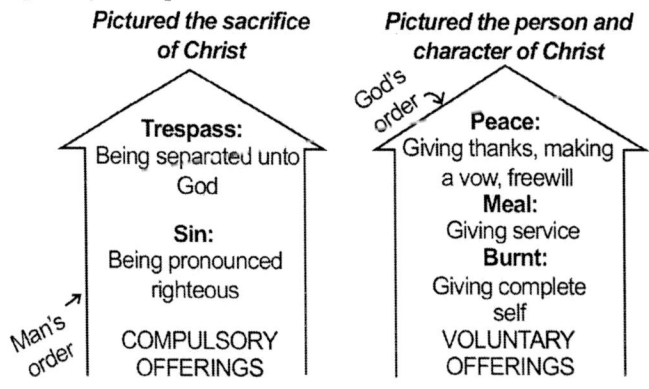

Each of the offerings pictures something about the Redeemer, Jesus Christ. The voluntary offerings pointed to His person, character, and obedience. The compulsory offerings pointed to the sacrifice it was necessary for Him to make for our sins. Each of the offerings also describes an aspect of our worship to God. For example, the odor of the burnt offering pleased God (Leviticus 1:9). In a similar way, God is pleased when we offer ourselves completely to Him (Romans 12:1).

Application

11 Match each offering named below (right side) with each phrase that describes what it dealt with or expressed (left side). Write the number in front of the phrase.

... **a** Service offered to God

... **b** Sins of ignorance

... **c** Neglect of a person's rights

... **d** Consecration

... **e** Thanksgiving

... **f** Vow

... **g** Freewill expression

... **h** No blood was shed

... **i** Represented man's labor

1) Sin
2) Trespass
3) Burnt
4) Peace
5) Meal

The Appointed Feasts and Seasons
(Read Leviticus 16, 23–25)

Objective 6. *Discuss how the special seasons related to people's experiences and relationship to God.*

God had a way of constantly reminding the Israelites that they were His special people, called to separation from sin and communion with Him. The five offerings, which we have just studied, were saying constantly get into a right relationship with God. The feasts and seasons were saying constantly order your life to keep right with God. The faithful observance of these feasts and seasons was a part of the people's covenant commitment (Exodus 20–24).

Seven feasts were celebrated during three annual observances. These feasts or festivals were so important that all Israelite men were required to attend them (Exodus 23:14–17). The following diagram gives these feasts and shows how each one is a picture of experiences believers have today.

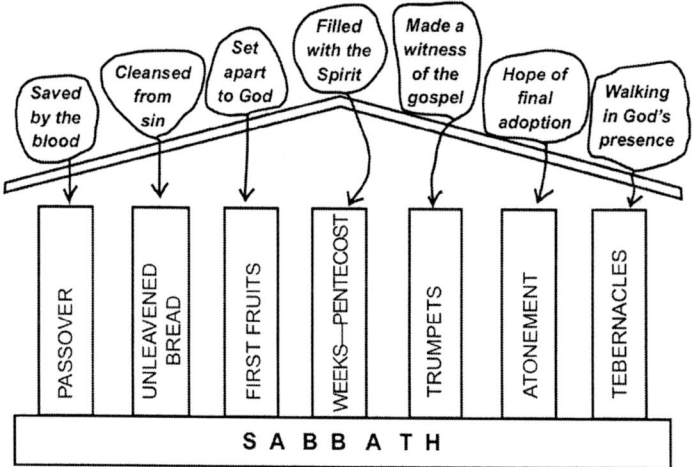

We may make the following observations:

1. The foundation of all experience in God is the Sabbath (Leviticus 23:1–3). Hebrews 4 teaches us that the believer can experience the Sabbath, or rest, by believing in God.

2. The seven feasts relate to seven experiences we may have in our walk in the Holy Spirit: being saved, cleansed, set apart or consecrated, filled, inspired to speak, adopted, and knowing God's presence.

Application

12 Match each feast (right side) to the phrase which describes its meaning for believers today (left side).

... **a** Living in God's presence

... **b** Accepted into God's family

... **c** Made clean from sin

... **d** Dedicated to God

... **e** Speaking forth the gospel

... **f** Saved through Christ's blood

... **g** Knowing the fullness of the Spirit

1) Passover
2) Unleavened bread
3) First fruits
4) Weeks—Pentecost
5) Trumpets
6) Atonement
7) Tabernacles

The Numbering and Organizing of the Camp (Read Numbers 1–10)

Objective 7. *State the spiritual principle illustrated by the organization of the camp of Israel.*

As shown in the book of Numbers, God gave Moses and Aaron instructions for taking a census. The tribes were numbered and arranged (Numbers 1–2), and the leaders, priests, and Levites were chosen and given their responsibilities. The following diagram shows how God gathered His people around Him. The twelve tribes guarded the tabernacle and were placed in their positions around it. The Levites (divided into the three families of the Merarites, Gershonites, and Kohathites) camped right next to the court. Moses and Aaron and the priest-family guarded the entrance. This entrance was the only way into the tabernacle and God's presence.

Some who have studied this description believe that the camp arranged in this way had a circumference of twelve miles. There were almost 3,000,000 people in perfect order with the cloud by day and the fire by night over the tabernacle (Numbers 9:15–23).

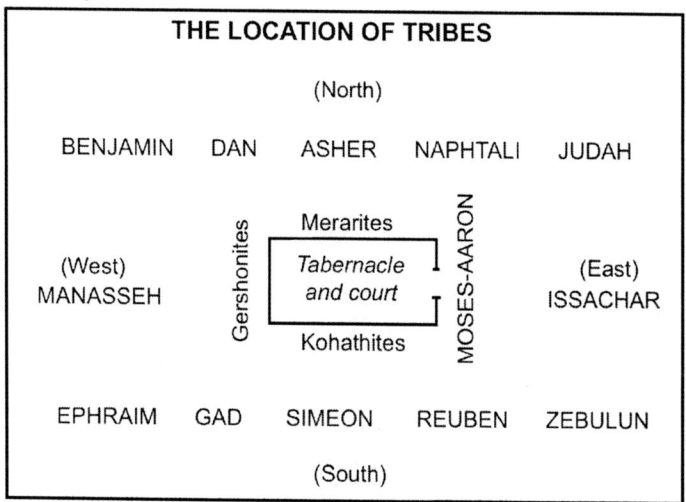

Application

13 The organization of the tribes around the tabernacle illustrated the principle or fact that
a) all of God's people have the same position and responsibilities.
b) God provided for order and organization among His people.
c) it was the leaders' idea to organize the people.
d) some people are not included in God's plan for organization.

GOD'S PEOPLE DOUBT AND WANDER

Objective 8. *Describe Israel's doubt and wandering and the spiritual lessons these events teach.*

After the year of preparation at Mt. Sinai, the Israelites marched for eleven days and reached Kadesh-barnea in the wilderness of Paran. They had marched in order as an organized unit. But the people were filled with complaining and rebellion (Numbers 11:1–35). There was jealousy among the leaders, even in Moses' family (Numbers 12:1–16). The doubt and unbelief of the people had serious consequences.

Application

14 Refer to the map at the beginning of this lesson. Circle the letter in front of each TRUE statement.
a) Kadesh-barnea is closer to Mt. Sinai than Rephidim is.
b) The wilderness of Paran is south of the wilderness of Shur.
c) Kadesh-barnea and the wilderness of Paran are both east of Egypt.

Delayed by Lack of Faith

Moses sent 12 spies into Canaan from the wilderness of Paran. They all reported that the land was good and that the people there were strong. Ten declared that it would be impossible to occupy Canaan and stirred the people to return to Egypt. However, two men, Joshua and Caleb, were confident that victory could be won. The people, unwilling to believe that God would give them the land, became a mob and resorted to stoning their leaders.

In judgment, God considered destroying the people. But Moses interceded again as he had done after the people had made the golden bull. Moses obtained a pardon for the people. The ten faithless spies died in a plague, and all the people aged twenty years and older (except Joshua and Caleb) were told that they could not go into Canaan. The people grieved but later rebelled by making an attempt to enter Canaan against Moses' orders. They were defeated and driven back by the Amalekites and Canaanites (Numbers 14:1–45).

History of Faith and Worship **105**

Application

15 Hebrews 3:16–4:7 refers to Israel's unbelief at Paran. In what way is their experience a warning to us today?
a) We should not disbelieve God's Word and refuse to have faith and act on it.
b) We should always expect God to give us a supernatural sign before we obey Him.
c) If some people we know doubt God's Word, we should wait until they believe before we obey God.

Learning While Delayed

The book we call Numbers is called *in the wilderness* or *desert journeys* in the Hebrew language. After they turned back from entering Canaan, the Israelites wandered in the desert for 39 years (Deuteronomy 2:14) until an entire generation died (Numbers 15:1–20:13). The accomplishment of God's purpose for them was delayed, but He continued to be faithful. He gave them food every day, guided them by the pillar of fire and the cloud, and accepted their sacrifices and worship in the tabernacle.

In Numbers 16:1–50 we read that Korah, Nathan, and Abiram led a great rebellion against Moses. As a result, they perished along with their families and 14,700 other Israelites. At this time God confirmed that He had chosen Aaron to serve as Priest. He caused Aaron's rod to blossom (Numbers 17).

Many other events are described in Numbers 15–22:1. The experience of the poisonous snakes (Numbers 21:6–9) showed the people that they needed faith. Anyone who looked at the bronze snake Moses had made and put on a pole was saved.

We can learn many lessons from the other events given in these chapters. God is kind and forgiving. He continues to lead us even when we miss His perfect will. But oh, how costly doubt is! Like the Israelites, we can allow our fear to keep us from enjoying God's full intention for us. We can feel as small as grasshoppers beside our problems like they did (Numbers 13:33). When we compare our difficulties to our own strength and forget God, our journey—like theirs—will be one of despair.

Application

16 Circle the letter of the statement which best describes the wilderness wanderings.
a) Because the people did not have faith, God left them to wander in the desert alone.
b) Although the people had doubted God, His presence did not leave them during their wanderings.
c) It did not matter that the people had doubted God because His presence stayed with them.

GOD'S PEOPLE HEAR FINAL INSTRUCTIONS

(Read Numbers 35, Deuteronomy 1, 7, 11–12, 27–28, 30, 34)

Objective 9. *Summarize the final instructions given by Moses in the book of Deuteronomy.*

After the forty years of wandering, Israel camped on the plains of Moab, east of the Dead Sea (also called the Salt Sea). Numbers 33:50–36:13 and the entire book of Deuteronomy record the final instructions they received before entering Canaan.

Moses gave his final message to the people about one month before they crossed the Jordan. He probably spoke it out loud, taking about seven days to do so. His audience was a new generation of Israelites, all under the age of sixty. His message occupies the entire book of Deuteronomy except the final chapter, which was probably written by Joshua. It can be divided into three addresses:

1. Deuteronomy 1–4: A survey of God's revelation to Israel

2. Deuteronomy 5–26: An exhortation to let love motivate them to obey God's law

3. Deuteronomy 27–33: Warnings and prophecy concerning their entry into Canaan

Moses' words in Deuteronomy 6:5 seem to sum up the meaning of what we have learned. They state what we have learned, what is the key to our relationship with God: "Love the Lord your God with all your heart and with all your soul and with all your strength." Love is the key to faith and worship of the true God. Love means commitment and involves a lifestyle of exclusive devotion. Love demands all the strength of heart and soul. It is possible for us to love in this way because this is how God loves us (compare 1 John 4:19). You should take special notice also of Deuteronomy 28:1–14. This is a remarkable statement of what the nation of Israel could be if they would obey God.

Jesus quoted from the book of Deuteronomy more frequently, and the New Testament writers refer to it more often than any other book in the Old Testament. Compare Matthew 4:1–11 and Luke 4:1–13 with Deuteronomy 8:3; 6:13, 16; and 10:20. Notice how Jesus used statements from this book when He was in conflict with the devil.

Application

17 Circle the letter of the phrase that best summarizes the content of the book of Deuteronomy.
a) Several speeches by Moses about different parts of Israel's history
b) Laws about the priesthood—the high priest, the robes, and the special ceremony of consecration
c) A review of God's dealings with Israel, a reminder of His laws, and instructions on living in Canaan

---

We have studied the history of the development of faith and worship among God's people after they were freed from slavery in Egypt. Moses, their mighty leader, was a grand old man at the end of the book of Deuteronomy—120 years old. Deuteronomy 32 records the song he sang for Israel. His disobedience at Kadesh (Numbers 20:10) meant that he could not enter Canaan. But God took him to mount Nebo and showed him the land. He died there on the mountain and God buried Moses, His servant. He had not only led God's people for forty years, but also is credited with writing one-fourth of all the literature known today as the Old Testament.

self-test

1 Match each of the three kinds of law God gave to Israel (right side) to each phrase that describes it (left side).

... **a** Rules for the nation
... **b** The Ten Commandments
... **c** Having to do with worship
... **d** Permanent in nature
... **e** Laws concerning marriage

1) Moral law
2) Civil Law
3) Ceremonial law

2 Following are several statements about the priesthood and its meaning. Circle the letter of each TRUE statement.
a) Any priest could enter the Holy of Holies.
b) God appointed priests because He wanted the people to worship Him in an orderly manner.
c) The Levites were chosen to be priests before the Israelites came to Mt. Sinai.

3 The offerings were of two kinds—compulsory and voluntary. Match each of these types (right side) to each phrase describing its meaning or what it included (left side).

... **a** Trespass and sin offerings
... **b** Pictured the sacrifice of the Son
... **c** Man's order began with
... **d** Peace, meal, and burnt offerings
... **e** God's order began with
... **f** Pictured the character of the Son
... **g** Had to do with service
... **h** Had to do with judgment on sin

1) Voluntary offerings
2) Compulsory offerings

4 According to Hebrews 4, those who enter God's rest (or Sabbath) are those who
a) believe what He has said.
b) do not work to provide their material needs.
c) keep all the Old Testament laws.

5 At Paran, the Israelites turned back from entering Canaan for
a) they were not prepared to go in.
b) God's presence had left them.
c) they did not believe God.
d) all the spies brought bad reports.

6 From the list below, select the five major ways in which God organized His people. Circle the letter in front of each one.
a) Moral law
b) Priesthood
c) Passover
d) Tabernacle
e) Sacrifices and offerings
f) Burnt sacrifices
g) Holy of Holies
h) Position of the tribes
i) Bronze altar
j) Feasts and seasons

7 Circle the letter in front of each TRUE statement.
a) Abraham became righteous in God's eyes by keeping the law.
b) God gave the law to Israel after He had already made a covenant with Abraham.
c) Though believers today do not keep the ceremonial law, it pictures many truths about worship.
d) The organization of the camp of Israel picture the way God expects people to come to Him.
e) The first time sacrifices were offered to God was by Moses at Mt. Sinai.

8 Match each truth concerning believers today (left side) with the item on the right which illustrates it best.

... **a** The church needs to have a definite order and organization.

... **b** Believers must live holy lives, separated from sin.

... **c** Only through Christ can we enter into God's presence.

... **d** The sacrifice of Christ is required to remove sin.

... **e** The foundation of a believer's experience is his or her belief in God.

1) Priesthood
2) Tabernacle
3) Camp of Israel
4) Sacrifices and offerings
5) Feasts and seasons

9 Put the following events into chronological sequence by numbering them from 1 to 8.

... **a** Jacob and his eleven sons went to live in Egypt along with Joseph.

... **b** The Israelites received the Law at Mt. Sinai.

... **c** Adam and Eve disobeyed God and were sent out of the Garden.

... **d** The Israelites wandered in the desert for 40 years.

... **e** Moses led the Israelites out of Egypt.

... **f** Noah and his family were saved from the Flood.

... **g** God destroyed mankind's plans to build the tower of Babel.

... **h** Abram (Abraham) left the city of Ur and went to Canaan.

Before you continue your study with Lesson 5, be sure to complete your student report for Unit 1 and return Answer Sheet 1 to your GU instructor.

answers to study questions

9 a 5) Altar of incense
  b 6) Ark of the covenant
  c 1) Altar of sacrifice
  d 3) Table of bread
  e 2) Bronze basin
  f 7) Mercy seat
  g 4) Lampstand

1 a) True
  b) False
  c) False
  d) True

10 Your answer. Two of the most important ways are these: 1) The need for holiness and consecration was illustrated by the ceremony of consecration and the laws of holy living (Leviticus 21:1–22:10); 2) The importance of acceptable worship was illustrated by the rules regarding the making of sacrifices (see for example Exodus 28:36–38).

2 Your answer. Suggested answer: To show that the covenant between God and His people was based on sacrifice and atonement for sin.

11 a 5) Meal
  b 1) Sin
  c 2) Trespass
  d 3) Burnt
  e 4) Peace
  f 4) Peace
  g 4) Peace
  h 5) Meal
  i 5) Meal

3 a 2) Law 5
  b 3) Laws 6, 7, 9
  c 1) Laws 1–4
  d 4) Laws 8, 10

12 a 7) Tabernacles
  b 6) Atonement
  c 2) Unleavened bread
  d 3) First fruits
  e 5) Trumpets
  f 1) Passover
  g 4) Weeks—Pentecost

4 Your answer should include at least one way you can apply each of the commandments to your life.

13 b) God provided for order and organization among His people.

5 b) The Law makes us realize our sinful condition and shows us we need God's righteousness.

14 a) False
  b) True
  c) True

6 b) numbering and organization of the tribes.

15 a) We should not disbelieve God's Word and refuse to have faith and act on it.

7 Your answer. It was portable because God wanted to dwell among His people wherever they journeyed.

16 b) Although the people had doubted God, His presence did not leave them during their wanderings.

8 See the discussion of the tabernacle and its furnishings.

17 c) A review of God's dealings with Israel, a reminder of His laws, and instructions on living in Canaan

Living in the Land

Lessons
- 5 A Home for the People of God
- 6 A Kingdom United
- 7 Writings of a Kingdom Age
- 8 A Kingdom Divided

LESSON 5: A Home for the People of God

God's people had been set free from their bondage in Egypt by the mighty hand of God. They had received God's instructions for organizing their life and worship according to His design. After the delay caused by doubt, they had assembled on the plains of Moab and listened to Moses' words. But then Moses died. Who would lead them into the land so that they could possess it?

As you study this lesson and read in your Bible of the events, you will become acquainted with the man God chose to lead His people forward. You will follow the people as they enter into the land and win many victories. You will also see them go through darkness and difficulty and see how God continued to guide them into fulfilling His purpose for them as a nation. He desired that their family life, worship, and prosperity be a witness of himself, the only true God, to all the peoples of the earth.

Your study of this lesson will help you understand the various experiences God's people had during the first years they possessed and lived in their land. As you understand these experiences, you can learn many lessons for your own life.

A Home for the People of God

lesson outline

The Leader and the Land
The Lessons Learned in Darkness
The Light Given for the Future

lesson objectives

When you finish this lesson you should be able to:

- Match descriptions of the events in Joshua's life to their importance in his preparation for leadership.

- Describe the physical features of the land of Palestine.

- Explain why Israel was commanded to conquer the land of Canaan.

- On a map of Palestine, identify the areas gained by the conquest.

- Identify facts about the area each tribe was given.

- Given a description of the cycle of judgment and deliverance, identify examples of it in the book of Judges.

- State the historical and spiritual significance of the book of Ruth.

- Show why God judged Eli.

- Describe Samuel's character and the nature of his leadership of Israel.

learning activities

1. Read from the books of Joshua, Judges, Ruth, and 1 Samuel as directed by the lesson.

2. Study the lesson development as usual, paying special attention to the maps and diagrams of Palestine. Answer the study questions, complete the self-test, and check all your answers.

key words

cross-section	inhabitant	parallel
cycle	inheritance	plateau
debauchery	invaders	successor
era	league	

lesson development

The diagram below outlines the major eras of Israel's history. This diagram shows the progression was upward to the kingdom era of David and Solomon as Israel increased in prosperity and success. Then the course was downward from the division of the kingdom to the Babylonian captivity.

We have already studied the *Exodus*. This lesson deals with the Conquest and the times of the *Judges*. In the rest of the lessons in this course you will study the events that take place during the remaining eras of the *Kingdom*, the *Two Kingdoms*, *Judah Alone*, and the *Captivity*.

Application

1 Study this diagram carefully and memorize it. Then without looking at it, draw it in your notebook with the seven steps and the name of the era each one represents.

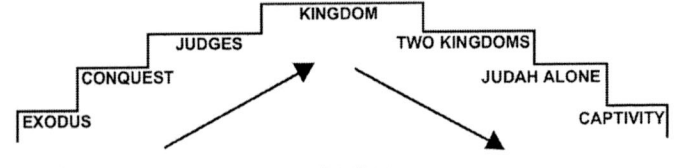

THE LEADER AND THE LAND

Joshua—His Preparation and Ministry

Read Joshua 1

Objective 1. *Match descriptions of the events in Joshua's life to their importance in his preparation for leadership.*

God had prepared a man to lead His people into the land of promise—Joshua, son of Nun, a man who had been chosen earlier to spy out Canaan. Caleb, another one of the spies, and Joshua were the only ones who had brought back a good report (Numbers 11:1–14:10). It was to Joshua that God said these words: "'Moses my servant is dead. Now then, you and all

A Home for the People of God **119**

these people, get ready to cross the Jordan River into the land I am about to give to them—to the Israelites'" (Joshua 1:2).

Application

2 In your Bible, read each of the Scriptures about Joshua given in the references below (right side). Then match it to the statement which best expresses its importance in Joshua's preparation to be the successor of Moses (left side).

.... **a** Was chosen by God to succeed Moses

... **b** Spent time in the Tent of the Lord's presence

... **c** Declared his faith and confidence in God in front of Israel

... **d** Had experience in helping Moses

... **e** Had his name changed from Hoshea ("salvation") to Joshua ("the Lord is salvation")

... **f** Was acknowledged by Moses as his successor in front of all the people

... **g** Had experience in leading a battle and defeating the enemy

1) Exodus 17:10–16
2) Exodus 33:11
3) Numbers 13:16
4) Numbers 14:5–10
5) Numbers 27:18
6) Numbers 27:22–23

Though Joshua's preparation can be followed in the books of Exodus and Numbers, it is in the book of Joshua that we read about his years as leader of the nation of Israel. We may divide the book of Joshua into two main parts:

1. Chapters 1–12 describe the conquest of Canaan;
2. Chapters 13–24 tell how the land was divided among the various tribes.

This book gives evidence of being a genuine historical account; some 300 cities and towns are mentioned in it. The events it describes took place over a time span of about 25 years. Joshua's final speech to Israel, which is recorded in chapters 23 and 24, shows the godly character of this man who trusted supremely in the Lord and relied upon Him.

Canaan—Its Description, Conquest, and Partition

The Features of the Land

Objective 2. *Describe the physical features of the land of Palestine.*

The land of Canaan was God's choice for His people. Learning some facts about it will help you understand the Scriptures better. The events that took place there will become more alive to you.

Canaan was named after the fourth son of Ham, who was the ancestor of its first inhabitants (Genesis 9:18). However, to avoid confusion, I will refer to the physical land itself as Palestine. During Old Testament times, the area of Palestine had an average width of 65 miles, measuring 100 miles at the widest part. Its greatest length was 180 miles. So it was no larger than a state or province in many countries today.

As the land God chose for His people, it had four special features.

1. *It was isolated.* A glance at the map will show that on the west was the sea, on the south and east were deserts, and on the north were mountains. This isolation was to help God's people to develop according to His plan. The nations surrounding Israel were idolatrous. But to Israel was given the revelation of the true God.

2. *It was central.* Although it was isolated, Palestine was located in the center of all the great powers of the ancient world. It was used as a land bridge for travel between them. The nations of Egypt, Babylon, Assyria, Persia, Greece, and Rome all grew around it, Israel's location was important because God had raised it up to be a witness to the world.

3. *It was limited.* The small size of the land made it unsuitable for anyone who had political ambitions. God did not call Abraham to simply be the founder of another nation, but to be the man through whom all the families of the earth would be blessed.

4. *It was fruitful.* Even the faithless spies saw the agricultural produce of Palestine. It was capable of producing all that God's people would need as long as they would walk in obedience.

Application

3 The feature of the land of Palestine which made it especially suited for a people who had a message to give to the world was its
a) isolation.
b) centrality.
c) limited size.
d) fruitfulness.

The land falls roughly into a pattern of four parallel strips:

1. A maritime or coastal plain on the shore of the Mediterranean Sea
2. A central range of mountains along the western edge of the Jordan Valley
3. The Jordan River Valley
4. The plateau and mountains of eastern Palestine, which stretch on the east side of the Jordan Valley from Mt. Hermon in the north to Mt. Hor in the South

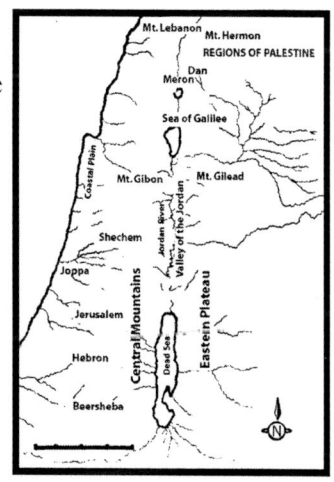

A diagram of a cross-section of the land looks like this:

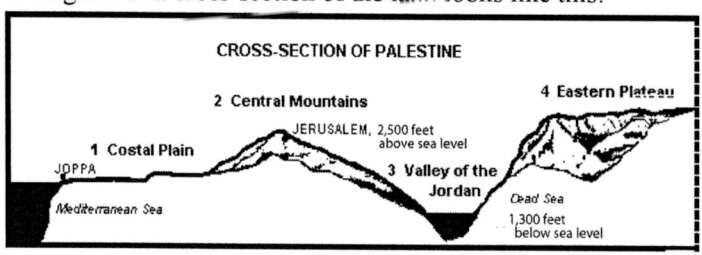

Application

4 Refer to the map and diagram, and circle the letter in front of each TRUE statement. Then in your notebook, rewrite each FALSE statement so that it is TRUE.

a) Jerusalem is north of Hebron.

b) Mount Gilead and Mount Gilboa are both located in the central mountainous range.

c) The Dead Sea is higher in elevation than the Mediterranean Sea.

d) The Jordan valley extends south from the Sea of Galilee to the Dead Sea.

e) The four main physical areas of the land of Palestine extend in parallel strips from east to west.

f) The coastal plain is lower than the plateau of eastern Palestine.

The Inhabitants of the Land

Objective 3. *Explain why Israel was commanded to conquer the land of Canaan.*

There were about seven tribes or nations occupying Canaan at the time Israel was ready to enter it. The Hittites were the most prominent and came from the formerly great empire of that name. They lived near Hebron in Abraham's time and later mingled with the Amorites in the mountains of what became Ephraim. The Canaanites lived on the sea coast, the Hivites near Shechem, the Perizzites in central and southern Palestine, the Girgashites near the Sea of Galilee, the Amorites in the eastern plateau, and the Jebusites in the central highlands around their capital which later became known as Jerusalem. The term "Canaanites" is often used to refer to all of these tribes or nations.

In Deuteronomy 20:16–18 God told the Israelites to destroy all the inhabitants of the land which He had given them. This command raises a serious question in many people's minds: How could a just God order Israel to do this? A great deal of misguided sympathy has been wasted upon the destruction of the Canaanites. Much more attention has been given to the judgment God sent upon them than to their character. As we study the Scriptures we find that there were reasons for God's command.

1. God knew that if these wicked nations were not destroyed they would teach Israel to sin against Him (Deuteronomy 18:9–13; Deuteronomy 20:18).

2. Canaan had been promised to Abraham and his children. Since the earth is the Lord's, He gives possession to whomever He pleases. When Jacob was dying in Egypt, he asked his sons to bury him in the land of Canaan as evidence of the hope that one day the promise would be fulfilled (Genesis 49:29–33).

3. Any right the Canaanites had to the land by having had possession of it for a long time was lost because of their wickedness. We must remember that these people also had descended from a godly line through Noah's sons. They were an example of a civilization which had followed the course described in Romans 1.

4. The moral depravity of the Canaanite peoples at this time demanded swift judgment. One writer of ancient history has said, "No other nation has rivaled the Canaanites in the mixture of blood and debauchery." Their life was so foul that 1500 years later in wicked Rome its practices were condemned. Sodom, where not even ten righteous men could be found, was an example of the cities of this civilization. The practices of the Canaanites are described in Leviticus 18:21–23 and Deuteronomy 12:30–32.

5. The driving out of the Canaanites is always shown in the Scriptures to be a punishment for their sins (Leviticus 18:24–25). The Israelites were warned that if they sinned and forsook their covenant with the Lord, they would suffer the same punishment (Joshua 23:11–13).

6. In His mercy, God had waited long for repentance among these nations. They had had the witness of righteous men

like Melchizedek (Genesis 14) and the patriarchs who lived among them. They had been warned by the destruction of Sodom and Gomorrah (Genesis 19:23–25). They had heard of the wonders by which the Israelites had been delivered from Egypt. They had even watched Israel's presence for almost forty years in the nearby desert.

Application

5 The Amorites, one of the Canaanite tribes, are mentioned in God's message to Abraham about the future of his descendants. Read Genesis 15:13–21 and answer the following questions.

a) How long would Abraham's descendants be slaves in a foreign land?

....

b) Why would it be this amount of time before Abraham's descendants would return to the land that was promised to them?

....

c) What does this show about God's attitude towards the people of the land?

....

6 Circle the letter in front of the statement which gives the main reason why God told Israel to conquer Canaan and destroy its inhabitants.

a) The Canaanites had no godly witness among them and were very wicked and immoral.
b) God had given the Canaanites time to repent, but they had continued in their sin.
c) The Israelites were more numerous than the Canaanites, and they deserved a good place to live.
d) After they left Egypt the Israelites had no land, so it was right for them to conquer Canaan.

A Home for the People of God

The Area of Conquest (Read Joshua 2–12)

Objective 4. *On a map of Palestine, identify the areas gained by the conquest.*

The people of Israel prepared to enter the land, following Joshua, the leader God had chosen for them. At this time Joshua was eighty years old. A great challenge lay ahead. The old civilizations were decaying. Could a new civilization based on a holy purpose to serve God be built? In Joshua 1:1–9 we read what God said to Joshua at this important time.

Application

7 Read Joshua 1:1–9. Then in your notebook answer the following questions.
a) What promises did God give to Joshua?
b) What advice did God give to Joshua?
c) According to verse 8, what three things did Joshua need to do in order to have success?

8 Read Joshua 3:7–17 and answer this question. What sign did the Lord perform to show Israel that He was with Joshua just as He had been with Moses?

The war of conquest took about seven years, and there were many difficulties. The cities were walled and great. There were leagues of kings and armed men with iron chariots. Yet the moral decay of the Canaanite tribes had produced a weakness in them like an internal disease.

Joshua's military campaign was well planned. It was a direct push for the heart of the land, cutting the Canaanite tribes into two parts. The Israelites moved quickly, and God was with them. Remember, this is not simply a history of a courageous people. It is an account of the powerful miracles of a covenant-keeping God!

The first area of conquest included the cities of Jericho, Ai, Bethel, Shiloh, Shechem, and Dothan. It included all the land west of these cities to about five miles from the Mediterranean Sea, and all of the land east to the other side of the Jordan.

The second area of conquest was to the south. It included the cities of Gibeon, Jerusalem, Jarmouth, Lachish, Eglon, Hebron, and Beersheba. It stretched west to within five miles of the Mediterranean Sea and east to within about five miles of the south end of the Dead Sea.

The third area of conquest was to the north. It included the cities of Beth-shan, Hazor, and Dan. It stretched east and west from about five miles east of the Jordan to within five miles of the Mediterranean Sea. It stretched north and south from about ten miles south of Beth-shan to ten miles north of Dan.

Application

9 On the following map, use your pencil to lightly outline each of these areas.

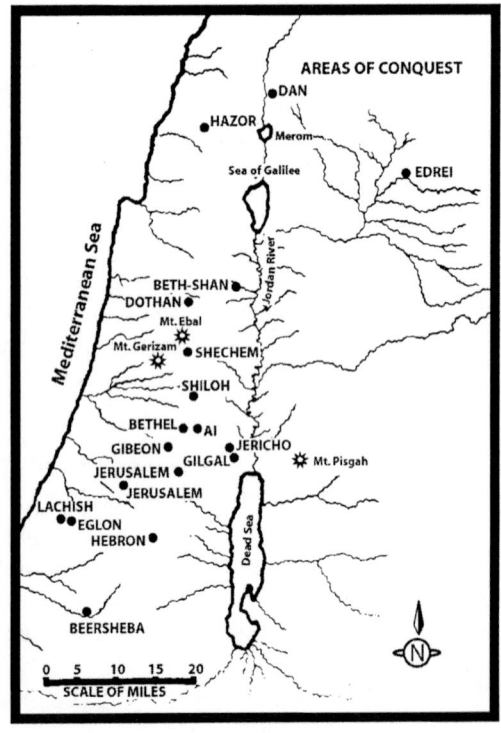

This war of conquest had far-reaching effects. We have received many benefits because of it, for it was from the little nation of Israel that the Bible and Jesus the Christ came. So the Israelites, in a sense, fought for us. Values we hold as precious were passed on to us from them: the worth of the individual, the importance of the home, and the worship of one God who is Creator and Father of all. We could almost say that the war they fought has had more effect on our lives than any other war that has been fought.

The Division of the Land (Read Joshua 13–24)

Objective 5. *Identify facts about the area each tribe was given.*

After the conquest of Canaan, each tribe was given a portion of land. This represented a spiritual as well as a physical inheritance. The Levites were given no land but received 48 cities with their suburbs. The total of 12 tribes was kept (since Levi was eliminated) by dividing the tribe of Joseph into the two sections of Ephraim and Manasseh. God's challenge to Joshua, "'There are still very large areas of land to be taken over'" (Joshua 13:1) was appropriate; the boundaries given in Joshua 13 were not realized until the time of Solomon, 500 years later. Study the following map and answer question 10.

Tents, Temples, and Palaces

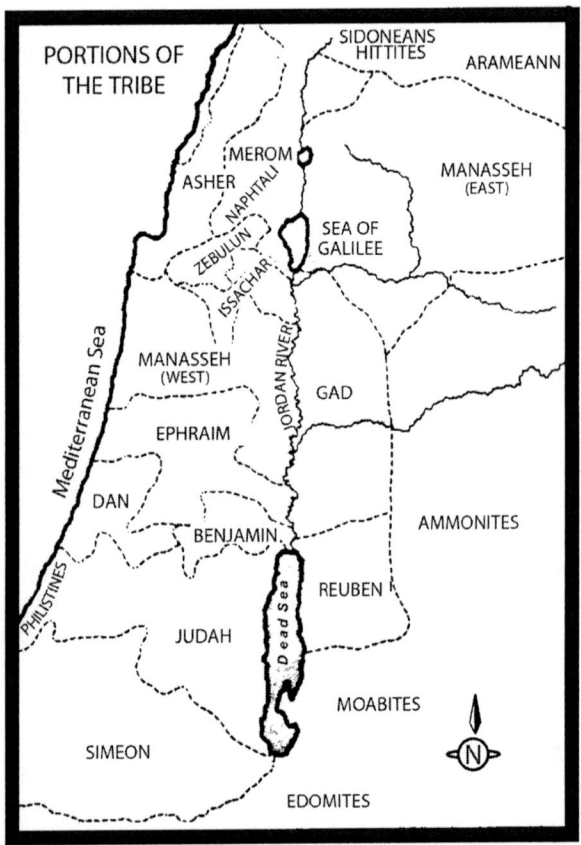

Application

10 Circle the letter in front of each TRUE statement below.
a) The tribe of Manasseh had an area about as large as that of Judah and Simeon combined
b) The tribe of Dan had two areas, both of them in the Jordan river valley.
c) The tribe of Asher shared its eastern border with that of Naphtali.
d) The tribe of Reuben was the furthest south on the west side of the Jordan river and the Dead Sea.

THE LESSONS LEARNED IN DARKNESS

God's people went through a difficult transition time after the death of Joshua until Samuel became their leader. This time of transition was one of change, adjustment, and rearrangement. It lasted about 400 years.

Judges—Cycles of Despair

Read Judges 1–16; 21

Objective 6. *Given a description of the cycle of judgment and deliverance, identify examples of it in the book of Judges.*

The period of transition we read about in the book of Judges was a time of great spiritual darkness of Israel. But though the book of Judges tells us about this very dark time in Israel's history, it is still part of the Bible canon. Its events are referred to in many other places in the Bible. The name *Judges* comes from the name given to the heroes of Israel whose deeds are the central theme of the book.

In general, Israel begins in humble dependence upon God (Judges 1:1–2:5) and then falls away into the depths of sin. The horrors described in the last four chapters show that the condition of Israel had reached the worst state imaginable.

You may ask, How could God's people sink so low? After Canaan was settled, the tribes seemed to fall apart. There was no central government and no single leader as there had been with Moses and Joshua. It seems that the eldership and priesthood failed to hold the tribes together in unity. There were also the problems of repelling invaders and keeping the land quiet.
God's Word gives some other simple and basic reasons which explain why this was such a dark time.

Application

11 Read each of the following verses of Scripture. Then in your notebook, write an answer to this same question for each one: What evil does it say that Israel committed?
a) Judges 1:27–28, 30–31, and 3:6
b) Judges 2:10
c) Judges 2:12
d) Judges 2:17, 19

12 Read chapters 17 and 21 of Judges. You will find that there is a verse in chapter 17 which is repeated in chapter 21. What do both of these verses say?

....

This description sums up the spirit of this era in Israel's history.

Throughout the book of Judges the same pattern or cycle was repeated several times; Judges 2:11–19 gives a general summary of this pattern. There were four main stages in the cycle each time.

1. Sin—Israel fell into sin and idolatry.
2. Punishment—God let their enemies overtake them.
3. Repentance—They cried out to the Lord.
4. Deliverance—The Lord raised up a judge to deliver them.

Application

13 Read Judges 2:11–19 and Judges 3:7–11, which is an example of this cycle. Then beside each stage listed below, give the references of the verses from Judges 3:7–11 in which it is found.

a) Sin..
b) Punishment......................................
c) Repentance.....................................
d) Deliverance....................................

A Home for the People of God

This cycle expresses a simple outline of God's dealing with Israel throughout the book of Judges. There are fourteen judges mentioned in the book (one of these, Abimelech, was not raised up by God). However, the thirteen separate administrations represented can be grouped into seven actual cycles of punishment.

Application

14 The seven cycles are given in the references below. Find and read the verses that describe each one. Then in your notebook, write each reference on the left-hand side. Opposite each reference, list the following: a) the name or names of the conqueror; b) the length of time Israel was ruled by the conqueror; c) the names of the judges God raised up to deliver Israel; and d) the length of time of rest that followed. The first is written in as an example.

Reference	Conqueror	Length	Judge	Time of Rest
1 3:1–11	Cushan Rishathaim	8 yrs.	Othniel	40 yrs.
2 3:12–31				
3 4:1–5:31				
4 6:1–8:32				
5 8:33–10:5				
6 10:6–12:15				
7 13:1–16:31				

Chapters 17 through 21 tell of other events that happened during this time. As we have mentioned already, they show to what depths of sin the nation had fallen. But there is also another story that took place during this time.

Ruth—Promise of Life

Read Ruth 1–4

Objective 7. *State the historical and spiritual significance of the book of Ruth.*

The beautiful and romantic story told in the book of Ruth concerns events that happened in the life of a simple Israelite family who lived during the period of the Judges (Ruth 1:1). The father made a decision to leave the land of promise during a famine. The results seemed terrible for his family. But the story of Ruth shows that God's hand of providence was upon His people in spite of their faithlessness as seen in the book of Judges.

The book of Ruth may be divided into three major sections.

1. Naomi and Ruth return to Bethlehem (1:1–22).

2. Ruth meets Boaz (2:1–3:18).

3. Boaz marries Ruth (4:1–22).

Application

15 Read the book of Ruth. Find the city of Bethlehem, the land of Judah, and the land of Moab on the map. Circle the letter in front of each TRUE statement.
a) Both Orpha and Ruth went to Bethlehem with Naomi.
b) Boaz was a relative of Ruth's husband, who had died.
c) The Moabites were one of the tribes of Israel who lived east of the Dead Sea.
d) Boaz allowed Ruth to gather grain from his fields.

But the book of Ruth is more than just a beautiful story. It is the Bible's clearest picture of the person whom Israelite law called the "kinsman-redeemer." When a man died, his nearest relative could make a claim for him since he could no longer act for himself. This man was called the kinsman-redeemer or the relative who brings back or restores. As we read Ruth's story we see that this is just exactly what Boaz did. Because he was Ruth's relative, he was able to restore to her the property belonging to Mahlon, marry her, and raise up a son to carry on the family line (Ruth 4:9–15). Boaz is thus a picture of Christ, our kinsman-redeemer.

Application

16 Boaz's position as Ruth's kinsman-redeemer best illustrates the fact that Christ
a) did all things according to the will of His father.
b) was related to us as a human being and as such could help us.
c) performed earthly miracles to demonstrate His divinity.
d) was proved to be God's Son by being raised from the dead.

17 Read Ruth 4:18–22 and Matthew 1:1–17. Circle the letter in front of the name of each person who descended from Ruth and Boaz.
a) Abraham
b) David
c) Noah
d) Christ
e) Judah
f) Isaac

Ruth, a gentile (non-Israelite), was outside of hope. Yet her decision to worship the true God (Ruth 1:16) placed her in a position to be in the line of Christ the Messiah. She represents all sinners who by faith become a part of the people of God.

THE LIGHT GIVEN FOR THE FUTURE

Eli—A Man Judged by God

Read 1 Samuel 1–4

Objective 8. *Show why God judged Eli.*

There are two additional judges in Israel—Eli and Samuel—who appear in the book of 1 Samuel. Eli held the office of both high priest and judge. He was a man of personal virtue. Yet he did not stop his sons from misusing their position as priests to commit great sin. The behavior of these sons, Hophni and Phinehas, show the awful condition of the priesthood at this time (1 Samuel 2:12–17). This condition caused the people to fall away from worshipping God, which was their only bond of national unity. Through a prophet, God warned Eli of the judgment coming upon his house (1 Samuel 2:27–36). God also warned him through the boy Samuel, who was being raised in the tabernacle, the tent of the Lord's presence (1 Samuel 3:10 18).

But Eli's sons continued in their evil ways, and God brought about the judgment of which Eli had been warned. The Philistines came against Israel at the battle of Aphek, the Ark of the Covenant was captured, Hophni and Phinehas were killed in battle, and Eli died when he received the news (1 Samuel 4:1–22).

Application

18 Find the land of the Philistines on the map and fill in the missing names in the sentence below.

The land of the Philistines had the tribe of ....

to the north, the tribes of .... and............

to the east, and the .... on the west.

19 Circle the letter in front of each statement which gives a reason why Eli and his family were judged by God.
a) Eli refused to take care of the boy Samuel.
b) Hophni and Phinehas would not let people bring sacrifices.
c) Eli misunderstood Hannah's distress at first.
d) Eli's sons treated the Lord's sacrifices with disrespect.
e) Eli allowed his sons to continue in their sin.

The victory of the Philistines brought about twenty years of oppression for Israel (1 Samuel 7:2–5). This twenty-year bondage, however, became one of the most important times for God's people. The judgment of God had fallen upon the priestly line of Eli. But God had raised up another leader, Samuel, who was eventually acknowledged by all Israel to be a prophet of the Lord (1 Samuel 3:19–21). The darkness of the time of oppression was turned to light because of the faithfulness of this man, the last judge of Israel.

Samuel—A Man Born for the Future

Read 1 Samuel 5–7

Objective 9. *Describe Samuel's character and the nature of his leadership of Israel.*

The name *Samuel* means "asked of God." He was born in response to the prayers of a devout but barren woman, Hannah. She gave him to the Lord to be raised at the tabernacle by Eli. God spoke in an audible voice to Samuel when he was still a child about the judgments that were to come upon the house of Eli. Samuel became one of the noblest men in Bible history, a man equal in greatness to Abraham, Moses, and David. He was a mighty man of prayer and faith. He became judge, reformer, statesman, and writer.

During the time of oppression by the Philistines, he challenged the people to return to the Lord with all their hearts. He called all Israel to meet him at Mizpah, and there the people repented and turned to God. When the Philistines attacked, God helped the Israelites to win a great victory.

Application

20 Read 1 Samuel 7:1–17 and answer the following questions in your notebook.
- **a)** What action did the Israelites take at Mizpah to demonstrate their repentance?
- **b)** What was Samuel doing when the Philistines attacked?
- **c)** What did Samuel say when the Philistines were defeated?
- **d)** What reminder of the victory did Samuel raise and what did he call it?

21 In your notebook, describe some occasion or time in your life when you realized, like Samuel did, that the Lord had helped you all the way.

After the victory against the Philistines at Mizpah, Samuel returned to his home at Ramah and built an altar (1 Samuel 7:17). It was probably during this time that Samuel founded schools for recruiting and training young men in the worship of God. In 1 Samuel 19:18–19 you will see the place Naioth in Ramah. *Naioth* is a word which suggests the idea of huts or dwellings where students could live. The phrase in Ramah also leads us to conclude that Samuel probably gave his own house over to the purpose of teaching. It was likely that he taught writing, law, and music, all directed towards the true worship of God. And no doubt he encouraged men to seek a prophetic word from God. In 1 Samuel 19:18–24 is a description of the powerful manifestation of the Lord's presence which was experienced at the school in Ramah.

It was probably at these schools that the Psalms first began to be written. David, for example, associated with the school in Ramah (1 Samuel 19). These schools were called schools of the prophets later on, and during the time of Elijah they existed at Bethel, Jericho, and Gilgal (2 Kings 2:1–5; 4:38–41).

Samuel grew old and made his sons judges. However, they did not follow his example and were very corrupt. It was at this time that Israel demanded a king, much to Samuel's disappointment (1 Samuel 8:1–9).

Application

22 Review this section on the life of Samuel and read the following Scriptures: 1 Samuel 3:10–18; 7:3–6, 15–17; 19:18–24. Then write a short description of the character of Samuel and his leadership in Israel.

self-test

1 Circle the letter in front of each TRUE statement.
a) The first battle in which Joshua participated was the seven-year war of conquest.
b) Moses had a special ceremony to show the people that Joshua would be his successor.
c) The second area of conquest was towards the south, taking in the city of Beersheba.
d) Because the land of Palestine was isolated, this made it impossible for Israel to communicate with other nations.
e) The tribe of Levi inherited a portion of land about the same size as that of the tribe of Reuben.

2 Suppose a friend were to say to you: "I think God was very cruel and unfair to command the Israelites to completely destroy all the inhabitants of Canaan." Which of the following statements would be the best reply?
a) The Canaanites had been in the land for many years. It was time for someone new to take over. And since Abraham settled in Palestine, it was natural for the nation which descended from him to have the right to return there.
b) God had given the Canaanites a chance to repent, but they continued their wicked ways. So God brought the judgment they deserved upon them by using the Israelites to destroy them. If Israel sinned, they would be judged in the same way.
c) The ancestors of the tribes of Israel had been promised the land of Canaan. So when Israel had been set free from the Egyptians, they had the authority to do whatever they wanted to when they came into the promised land.

3 In the book of Judges each time after the Lord delivered the Israelites from their oppressors they
a) turned away from their sin.
b) continued to serve the Lord.
c) forgot the Lord and served idols.

4 Circle the letter in front of each conclusion we can draw from the events recorded in the book of Judges.
a) God had great patience with the Israelites and raised up many judges to deliver them time after time.
b) God is unforgiving because He allowed the Israelites to be punished and overrun by their enemies.
c) It was not important to God that the Israelites sinned as long as they eventually repented.
d) The judges needed God's help and direction to deliver Israel from oppression.
e) After the people had sinned God did not pay attention to their cry for deliverance.

5 Boaz was able to restore to Ruth her property and give her a place among the Israelites because he
a) was her near relative.
b) loved her and wanted to help.
c) knew about her family.

6 One of the important values of the story of Ruth and Boaz is that it is a beautiful illustration of Christ as the
a) sinless one who suffers.
b) near kinsman who restores.
c) perfect sacrifice which is offered.
d) divine Son who experiences death.

7 According to Ruth 4:13–22., Ruth was David's
a) mother.
b) grandmother.
c) great-grandmother.

8 Of which of the following principles would the story of Eli and his family be the best example?
a) God is very patient with sinners and those who disobey Him.
b) A person who turns from his sin will experience God's mercy.
c) When God's people cry out to Him for help, He hears them.
d) God expects parents to correct and discipline their children.

9 Match the name of the leader of Israel (right side) to each phrase which describes him (left side). If a phrase applies to both leaders, write 3 in front of it.

... **a** Called Israel to repent at Mizpah

... **b** Set up a memorial stone called "Stone of Help"

... **c** Led Israel across the Jordan river

... **d** Spent time in the Tent of the Lord's Presence

... **e** Was the leader of the prophets at Ramah

... **f** Lived before the times of the judges

... **g** Showed faith and trust in God

1) Joshua
2) Samuel
3) Both

answers to study questions

12 There was no king in Israel and everyone did as he pleased (or a similar answer).

1 Your diagram should look like the one in the lesson.

13 a) Verse 7
   b) Verse 8
   c) Verse 9
   d) Verses 9–11

2 a) 5) Numbers 27:18
   b) 2) Exodus 33:11
   c) 4) Numbers 14:5–10
   d) 2) Exodus 33:11
   e) 3) Numbers 13:16
   f) 6) Numbers 27:22–23
   g) 1) Exodus 17:10–16

14 Your chart should look like this:

Reference	Conqueror	Length	Judge	Time of Rest
1 3:1–11	Cushan Rishathaim of Mesopotamia	8 yrs.	Othniel	40 yrs.
2 3:12–31	Eglon, king of Moab and the Philistines	18 yrs.	Ehud, Shamgar	80 yrs.
3 4:1–5:31	Jabin, king of Canaan	20 yrs.	Deborah, Barak	40 yrs.
4 6:1–8:32	Midianites	7 yrs.	Gideon	40 yrs.
5 8:33–10:5	Civil war, etc.	not given	Abimelech, Tolar, Jair	not given
6 10:6–12:15	Ammonites	18 yrs.	Jephthah, Ibzan, Elon, Abdon	not given
7 13:1–16:31	Philistines	40 yrs.	Samson	20 yrs.

3 b) centrality.

A Home for the People of God

15 a) False
  b) True
  c) False
  d) True

4 a) True
  b) False; Mount Gilead is located in the plateau of eastern Palestine, and Mount Gilboa is located in the central mountainous region.
  c) False; the Dead Sea is lower in elevation than the Mediterranean Sea.
  d) True
  e) False; the four main physical areas of the land of Palestine extend in parallel strips from north to south.
  f) True

16 b) was related to us as a human being and as such could help us.

5 a) 400 years
  b) Because by that time the Amorites would have become so wicked that it would be necessary for God to drive them out.
  c) He was patient with them but one day His patience would come to an end if they continued in their wickedness.

17 b) David
  d) Christ

6 b) God had given the Canaanites time to repent, but they had continued in their sin.

18 Dan, Judah, Simeon, Mediterranean Sea

7 a) God promised Joshua 1) His presence, 2) continued victory, 3) the entire land, and 4) leadership of Israel. (Your answer should be similar to this.)
  b) God advised Joshua to 1) be determined and confident, 2) be sure to obey, read, and study the whole Law, 3) remember that God had commanded him to be determined and confident, and 4) not be afraid or

discouraged. (Your answer should be similar to this.)
   c) Joshua needed to read the book of the law, study it day and night, and obey everything written in it

19 d) Eli's sons treated the Lord's sacrifices with disrespect.
   e) Eli allowed his sons to continue in their sin.

 8 He caused the Jordan to cease flowing while the Israelites crossed.

20 a) They got rid of their idols and worshipped the Lord.
   b) He was offering a sacrifice to God.
   c) "'Thus far has the Lord helped us.'"
   d) A memorial stone which he called "stone of help."

 9 The areas on your map should correspond or be similar to this one.

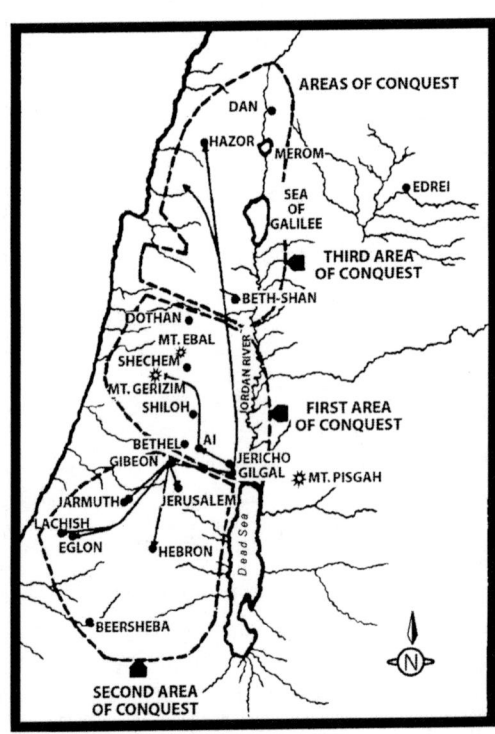

10 a) True
   b) False
   c) True
   d) False

22 Your answer should include the following ideas. Samuel obeyed the Lord and told Eli the message God had given him. He called the people to repentance at Mizpah, won a victory over the Philistines, and was recognized as a prophet of the Lord. He was a ruler and judge in Israel, and the leader of the prophets at Ramah.

11 a) They did not drive out the Canaanites but intermarried with them and worshipped their god.
   b) They forgot the Lord and what He had done.
   c) They stopped worshipping the Lord and began to worship other gods.
   d) They disobeyed their leaders and worshipped other gods.

LESSON 6: A Kingdom United

Under the leadership of Joshua, God's people entered the land of Palestine. They made many conquests and settled there. Then they went through a troublesome period of transition under the judges. Times were difficult, but God raised up leaders to deliver Israel from their oppressors. It was during this time that the last judge—Samuel—became Israel's leader.

It was Samuel who anointed Saul, Israel's first king. Saul's reign marked the beginning of the kingdom era. This era of the united kingdom continued through two more kings, David and Solomon. Each of these three kings ruled for about forty years.

The kingdom era was the most brilliant of Israel's history. The dark ages we have studied became a golden age. It was a time when God's promise was fulfilled. Israel took its place among the nations of the world. Its buildings, writings, and prosperity showed forth God's blessing for all the world to see! In this lesson you will learn about this marvelous time of blessing and prosperity and about the first three kings who ruled Israel.

A Kingdom United

lesson outline

The Idea of Kingship
The Reign of Saul
The Reign of David
The Reign of Solomon

lesson objectives

When you finish this lesson you should be able to:

- Summarize God's instructions and warnings concerning Israel's kingship.
- Summarize the major events in Saul's life.
- Identify facts connected with the four basic periods of David's life.
- State the reasons for Solomon's success and failure as king of Israel.

learning activities

1. Read from 1 Samuel 8 through 1 Kings 11 as the lesson directs you.
2. Carefully study the map and illustrations given in the lesson. Study the lesson as usual. Be sure to read the objectives and review the material until you can fulfill each one. Answer the studzy questions and the self-test, checking your answers. Remember to make use of the glossary.

key words

alliance	kingdom	reign
anointed	obligation	theocracy
conviction	prosperity	transition
dethroned.		

lesson development

THE IDEA OF KINGSHIP

Read 1 Samuel 8

Objective 1. *Summarize God's instructions and warnings concerning Israel's kingship.*

God's Instructions

Israel had not had a man as king until this time, for Jehovah had been their king! They had a *theocracy,* or a "government by God." The idea of a theocracy, in which God ruled through His appointed leaders, had not failed. The people, however, were unable to appreciate its benefits.

Although it was not His perfect will for Israel, God allowed them to have a king. He had foreseen the day when they would want one. Before they came into Palestine, He had given them instructions concerning how their kings should behave.

Application

1 Read Deuteronomy 17:14–20. In your notebook answer the following questions:
a) Who was the king to be?
b) What was the king to do?
c) What was the king not to do?

We may summarize these instructions by stating the following four principles:

1. The kings of Israel were not to rule by their own will.

2. They were not to rule for their own honor or glory.

3. They were to be concerned about the will of God and His direction for the good of the people.

4. The king was to be as much the subject of Jehovah as the humblest Israelite.

In all the future reigns of the kings in Israel these principles operated. As long as a king was dependent upon the will of God, he prospered. When a king made a practice of disobeying God's will he was ultimately dethroned.

The People's Demand

The people of Israel saw the nations around them and felt disunified and powerless in contrast. Also, Samuel's sons were evil and the elders wanted some way to avoid having them become Israel's leaders (1 Samuel 8:1–5). The Israelites gathered at Ramah, Samuel's home, and demanded to have a king. Their impatience, lack of trust, and rebellion was a grievous sin, and Samuel sought the Lord in sorrow. While God wanted Israel to be His special people, they wanted to be like the nations around them (1 Samuel 8:5, 19–20). Their request for a king showed that they did not trust God to protect them, as Samuel pointed out later (1 Samuel 12:6–12). God reminded Samuel, "'It is not you they have rejected, but they have rejected me as their king'" (1 Samuel 8:7).

Application

2 Why did God say to Samuel that He, not Samuel, was the one whom they had rejected?

....

God's Warning

God then directed Samuel to warn the people of the results of their choice to have a king.

Application

3 Read 1 Samuel 8:10–22 and compare it to Deuteronomy 17:14–20. In your notebook, answer the following questions with one or two sentences in your own words.

a) According to God's instructions in Deuteronomy 17:14–20, what was to be the king's main obligation? If the king fulfilled this obligation, what results would follow?

b) According to the warning God gave through Samuel in 1 Samuel 8:10–22, what would be the king's principal activity? What result would follow?

After the people had been warned of the consequences of their action, they still insisted on having a king. Then God told Samuel to go ahead and give them one (1 Samuel 8:19–22). When Saul had been anointed as king, Samuel gave his last message to Israel as their leader (1 Samuel 12). In his message he asked them to agree that his conduct had been blameless, which they did (vv. 3–5). He reminded them of what the Lord had done for them and told them again that they had sinned in mistrusting the Lord and asking for a king (vv. 6–12).

The people were fearful at his words and at God's miraculous confirmation of them which followed. They cried to Samuel, "'Pray to the Lord your God for your servants so that we will not die, for we have added to all our other sins the evil of asking for a king'" (v. 19). Samuel reassured the people and told them to serve the Lord. The principles which he stated formed a prophecy concerning all the kings which were to rule: "'Fear the Lord and serve him faithfully with all your heart; consider what great things he has done for you. Yet if you persist in doing evil, both you and your king will be swept away'" (vv. 24–25).

Though Samuel was no longer to be Israel's official ruler, he still was to have a great influence on the nation. The people sensed their need for his help, and Samuel responded gracious and beautiful manner (vv. 19–23).

Application

4 Read 1 Samuel 12:23. What did Samuel promise to do?

....

Has the Lord reminded you of people for whom you should pray? Perhaps they, like the people of God during Samuel's time, have strayed away from the Lord. We should follow Samuel's example and not sin against God by ceasing to pray for them.

Application

5 In your notebook, write down the names of any people for whom you should pray. You may want to look at this list from time to time to remind you to pray for them.

THE REIGN OF SAUL

Read 1 Samuel 9–15

Objective 2. *Summarize the major events in Saul's life.*

Chosen as King

Although the people did not choose a king by electing one, it is obvious that God picked one based on their desire. Saul was a handsome man in the prime of life, "an impressive young man without equal among the Israelites—a head taller than any of the others" (1 Samuel 9:2). He was the people's idea of a king.

After God revealed to Samuel that Saul would be king (1 Samuel 9:15–17), Samuel anointed him in a private ceremony (vv. 27–10:1). Samuel told Saul about the signs God would give him to confirm this choice and told Saul to wait for him at Gilgal. The signs came to pass as Samuel had prophesied. Then at Mizpah, after reminding the Israelites of their sin in asking for a king, Samuel publicly declared Saul to be king (1 Samuel 10:1–27).

Application

6 Read 1 Samuel 10:9. In what way did God display His grace and help toward Saul?

....

Victories and Failures

As commander of Israel's armies, Saul was a brilliant leader. He won victory after victory. But Saul could not bring himself under the authority of God. This failure ultimately caused God to reject him as king.

Application

7 In your notebook, make a chart like the following. Then read in your Bible the Scriptures which are listed. Under the appropriate heading, list the reference of each Scripture that belongs under it. Opposite the reference, write a brief description of the victory or failure. The first one is done as an example.

a) 1 Samuel 11:1–15
b) 1 Samuel 13:8–13
c) 1 Samuel 14:1–23
d) 1 Samuel 15:1–7
e) 1 Samuel 15:8–23

Saul's Victories		Saul's Failures	
Reference	*Description*	*Reference*	*Description*
1 Samuel 11:1–15	Defeated the Ammonites		

You may want to add other Bible references and descriptions to your chart as you continue to read about events in Saul's life.

Rejected as King

After Saul's disobedience at Gilgal (1 Samuel 13:8–12), Samuel told him for the first time that he and his family would not continue to rule Israel. "'The Lord has sought out a man after his own heart and appointed him leader of his people, because you have not kept the Lord's command'" (1 Samuel 13:14). After Saul's second disobedience, Samuel repeated his statement, now in stronger language:

> "Does the LORD delight in burnt offerings and sacrifices as much as in obeying the voice of the LORD? To obey is better than sacrifice, and to heed is better than the fat of rams. For rebellion is like the sin of divination, and arrogance like the evil of idolatry. Because you have rejected the word of the LORD, he has rejected you as king." (1 Samuel 15:22–23).

As Saul's life went on, he frequently admitted his sin but never really changed.

Application

8 The main reason Saul was rejected as king was because he
a) did not think it was necessary for him to completely obey the Lord.
b) spared the life of one of the kings whose city he had captured.
c) offered burnt and fellowship sacrifices to the Lord.

Saul's rejection was a great grief and disappointment to Samuel (1 Samuel 15:35). But God had another man in mind.

THE REIGN OF DAVID

Objective 3. *Identify facts connected with the four basic periods of David's life.*

The prophet Samuel prepared the way for David, Israel's greatest king. David had spent much of his youth as a shepherd, and these experiences form the background for many of the psalms he wrote which are recorded in the book of Psalms. But David did not remain a shepherd, for he was the man God had chosen to be a king.

Anointed as King

Read 1 Samuel 16:1–13

God stirred Samuel from his mourning over Saul and sent him to Bethlehem to the family of Jesse. David was Jesse's youngest son.

Application

9 Read 1 Samuel 9:2, 10:23, and 16:1–13. In your notebook, answer the following questions.
a) What did Saul and Eliab have in common?
b) Why did God reject Eliab?
c) What did God's choice of David indicate about him?

Samuel anointed David, and the Spirit of God took possession of him from that time on (1 Samuel 16:13).

Awaiting God's Time

Read 1 Samuel 16:14–23; 17:1–31:13; 2 Samuel 1

But several years passed before David actually became king of Israel. At first, David was associated with Saul's court, where his musical ability soothed the spiritually troubled king (1 Samuel 16:14–23).

Application

10 Read 1 Samuel 16:14–23. In your notebook, describe in your own words Saul's condition at this time.

David displayed his courage and trust in the Lord by answering the challenge of Goliath the Philistine (1 Samuel 17:20–58). His victory brought him to the attention of the people of Israel, and his popularity with them caused Saul to become jealous (1 Samuel 8:6–9). But none of the plans that Saul made to destroy David were successful. David married Michal, Saul's daughter, and became close friends with Jonathan, his son.

As David's military successes increased, so did Saul's jealousy of him. Saul knew the Lord was with David (1 Samuel 18:12, 28). Finally, David was forced to become an outlaw, fleeing from Saul's efforts to kill him (1 Samuel 19:11–17). The prophet Gad (whom David had probably already met among the prophets who were with Samuel at Ramah) was associated with him during this time and later on as well (1 Samuel 22:5; 2 Samuel 24:11–25).

At first David sought refuge in the kingdom of Israel. Later he fled to the nation of Gath to King Achish (1 Samuel 21). When he returned to Israel he took refuge in the cave of Adullam (1 Samuel 22) where many men gathered to him. After the prophet Samuel died and was buried at Ramah, David went to Paran (1 Samuel 25:1). Finally, after many narrow escapes, he made his headquarters at Ziklag (1 Samuel 27) where he remained until Saul's death.

During these years of exile and danger, David chose to submit himself to God's will.

Application

11 Read 1 Samuel 24 and 26. Why did David refuse to kill Saul when he had a chance to do so?

. . . .

In his submission to God's will, David represented the true ideal of kingship. Saul was just the opposite. His willful rebellion ultimately led him even into witchcraft (1 Samuel 15:23; 28:3–25). The closing years of Saul's reign were a struggle between the wayward king and God. Finally, in a terrible moment of defeat, Saul died by his own hand on Mount Gilboa. Three of his sons including Jonathan, David's closest friend, had already been killed in the battle with the Philistines. It was a tragic end to the career of Israel's first king. David's moving lament for Saul and Jonathan is recorded in 2 Samuel 1.

Ruling Over Judah
Read 2 Samuel 1–4

After Saul's death, only the tribe of Judah recognized David as king. He was anointed by them and reigned over Judah from Hebron for seven years (2 Samuel 1–4). Ishbosheth, Saul's son, reigned over the rest of the tribes, which were collectively called "Israel." But whereas David's family and descendants grew stronger, Saul's grew weaker. The two parts of the kingdom came into conflict with each other. Then, in a series of violent events, Ishbosheth was murdered by two of his own captains.

Ruling Over All Israel
Read 2 Samuel 5–24; 1 Kings 1:1–2:12

After the death of Ishbosheth, the tribes all gathered at Hebron and anointed David as king over all of Israel and Judah (2 Samuel 5:1–5). David took Jerusalem from the Jebusites who lived there, and established it as the capital of the united kingdom (2 Samuel 5). He reigned there for 33 years.

David continued to show his submission to God's desires. His first act was to bring back the Ark of the Covenant and place it in the capital city (2 Samuel 6). You remember that this symbol of God's presence had been lost at the battle of Aphek by Eli's godless sons, and then returned by the Philistines because of God's judgment upon them. The Israelites, also in fear, had kept it in a barn at a place called Kiriath Jearim. Although this place was only 8 miles west of Jerusalem, the ark had remained there for more than 20 years (1 Samuel 5–7), including all of Samuel's time as judge, all of Saul's years as king, and part of David's reign.

Application

12 Read 2 Samuel 7:1–29. Circle the letter of each TRUE statement.
a) God asked David to build a house for the Ark of the Covenant.
b) David promised God he would build a house for the Ark of the Covenant.
c) God told David that one of his sons would build a house for the Ark of the Covenant.

It was at this time that God made His covenant with David, promising him an everlasting kingdom. As time went on, David extended Israel's borders by making foreign conquests. He defeated the Philistines, the Moabites, and the Ammonites (2 Samuel 8–10).

Application

13 Compare the boundaries of David's kingdom as shown on the following map to the boundaries of the land when it was divided among the tribes as shown by the area which is shaded. About how much larger was David's kingdom?

....

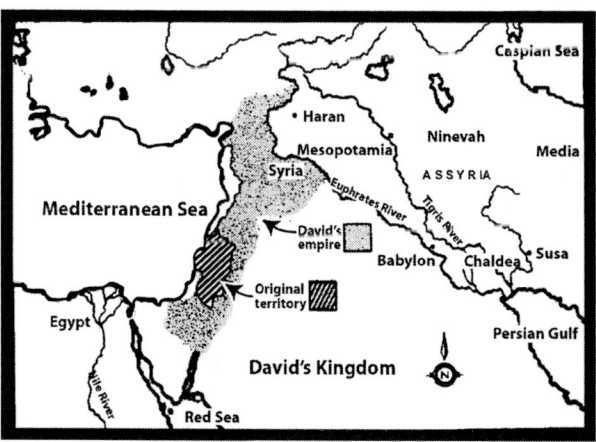

At the height of his success, David fell into terrible sin. He committed adultery with Bathsheba and arranged for her husband, Uriah, to die in battle (2 Samuel 11). Uriah had been David's associate and military captain for a long time. David's sin was brought to his attention by the prophet Nathan, and God's judgment was announced. The child Bathsheba bore to David died (2 Samuel 12:15–23). David sincerely repented and was forgiven by God and because of his humility and brokenness, God continued to use him. David wrote Psalms 32 and 51 at this time of conviction.

Application

14 Read Psalms 32 and 51. In your notebook, answer the following questions.
a) How did David respond to God's conviction in his life?
b) Has the Lord convicted you of something in your life? How have you responded?

God then, as though to prove to David His complete forgiveness, gave him and Bathsheba (who was now his wife) another son. This child was called Solomon, and it was he who became the next king of Israel (2 Samuel 12:24–25; 1 Kings 1:39–40).

But though David repented, the results of his sin were seen in his family. Most notable was the outbreak of wicked behavior among the sons of his different wives, such as Amnon's rape of his half-sister, Tamar, and Absalom's subsequent murder of Amnon (2 Samuel 13–14). Finally, there came the attempt of Absalom to overthrow his father. David was even driven from his throne for a short time by Absalom (2 Samuel 15–18). He was then restored to his kingdom (2 Samuel 19–20), and in a wonderful psalm of thanksgiving he honored God (2 Samuel 22–23).

David sinned again by numbering his people. This showed that he was trusting in the number of soldiers he had, not in the Lord. A plague was sent to Israel. After David's repentance and intercession, the plague was stopped, and David built an altar to the Lord on the threshing floor which belonged to a man named Araunah (2 Samuel 24:10–25).

As David reached the end of his life, one of his sons, Adonijah, tried to claim the throne. He was prevented from doing so, however, and Solomon became king. David died and was buried (1 Kings 1:1–2:12). As Israel's history unfolded, it was to his reign and his devotion to God that all other kings were compared.

Application

15 Review this section on the life of David. Then match each event (left side) with the period of David's life during which it took place (right side).

... **a** He reigned from Hebron.

... **b** He refused to kill Saul.

... **c** He brought the Ark of the Covenant.

... **d** He was brought to the palace to play music for Saul.

... **e** God made a covenant with him.

... **f** Samuel anointed him as king.

... **g** He won a victory over Goliath.

... **h** Saul's son Ishbosheth was murdered.

... **i** His son Absalom rebelled against him.

1) Anointed as king
2) Awaiting God's time
3) Ruling over Judah
4) Ruling over all Israel

THE REIGN OF SOLOMON

Read 1 Kings 2:13–11:43

Objective 4. *State the reasons for Solomon's success and failure as king of Israel.*

Obedience and Success

During the reign of Solomon, God brought Israel to a magnificence that astounded the world. Solomon ruled for 40 years (1 Kings 11:42) and began in greatness. When God asked him what he would like to have, he requested wisdom to rule God's people. This request pleased the Lord (1 Kings 3:5–14) and Solomon became known for his wisdom (1 Kings 3:28; 4:29–34). He trusted and loved God (1 Kings 3:3).

During his reign, many sacred songs and writings were produced. Solomon alone wrote 3,000 proverbs, of which some 375 are preserved in the Old Testament. He also wrote 1,005 songs, three of which are in the Bible (Psalms 72 and 127, and the Song of Solomon).

Four of the eleven chapters which tell about Solomon's kingdom are given to a description of the temple he built (1 Kings 5–8). This temple, which was built at Jerusalem on the same place where David had built his altar (2 Samuel 24), amazed the world. Its value in today's currency would be incalculable! The labor force alone included 30,000 Jews and no less than 153,000 Canaanites.

Application

16 Read the description of the temple in 1 Kings 5–8 and study the following illustrations which represent how it may have looked. Then review the description of the Tabernacle (also called the Tent of the Lord's Presence) in Lesson 4. In your notebook, list three ways the temple and the Tent were alike and the one main way in which they were different.

A Kingdom United

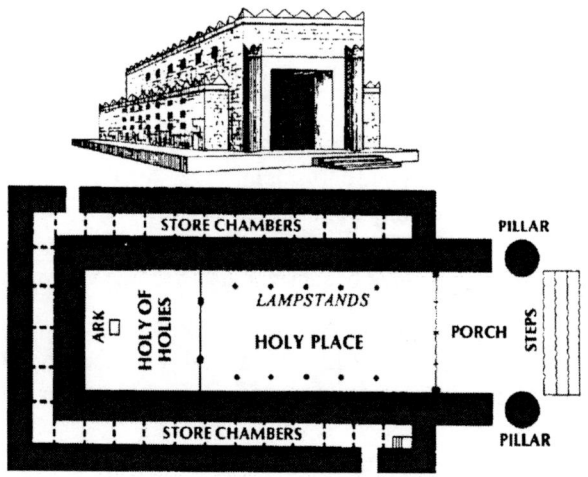

17 After Solomon built and dedicated the temple, God appeared to him again. Read 1 Kings 9:1–9. In your notebook, describe in your own words what God said would happen to the temple if Solomon or his descendants worshipped other gods.

During those years of Solomon's reign, the kingdom of Israel was an illustration of God's desire to bless His people, the people with whom He had made a covenant. The description we read in 1 Kings 10:14–29 suggests how great that kingdom was. God's people with His glory upon them were a wonder for the world!

Disobedience and Failure

But in spite of all of Solomon's success, he failed in his devotion to God. His kingdom increased in wealth and fame. He made alliances with foreign nations and married many wives from outside Israel, although God's command was against a king having many wives (Deuteronomy 17:17). Solomon's wives led him away from his father's God (1 Kings 11:1–8). He worshipped other gods, and the Lord judged him because of his disobedience.

Application

18 Read 1 Kings 11:9–11. Then circle the letter in front of each TRUE statement.
a) God said he would leave two tribes for Solomon's son for the sake of David and Jerusalem.
b) Solomon's kingdom would be taken away during the reign of his son.
c) Solomon was judged because he had become very rich.

19 Review this section on the reign of Solomon and read 1 Kings 3:3 and 11:1–2. Which of the following statements is the best description of the reasons for Solomon's success then failure as king?
a) As Solomon gained wealth and power he became successful. But it was these same blessings which later turned him away from the Lord.
b) As the son of king David, Solomon was promised great and lasting success. But this desire for wisdom became too strong and he failed.
c) In his first years as king, Solomon loved and obeyed the Lord. But later he married many foreign wives and began to worship their gods.

Solomon behaved like the tyrannical kings who ruled in the surrounding nations. When he died, the kingdom which had risen to such greatness was on the decline. Nevertheless, the glory and wealth of his kingdom are an example of the abundant blessings God wants to give His people.

self-test

1 Which is the best summary of God's instructions and warnings concerning kingship?

a) His instructions were that the king's main task was to be the spiritual leadership of the people. His warning was that unless the king brought a large group of priests into his household, he would be unable to rule the people.

b) His instructions were that the king was to obey His law completely and allow nothing to turn him aside from doing this. His warning was that the king would take from the people to build his own household and that the people would complain bitterly.

c) His instructions were that the king was to be responsible for building Him a temple and gathering a large army for Israel's protection. He warned that unless the king had a powerful group of soldiers his kingdom would be taken away.

2 Match each event (left side) to the king with whom it is associated (right side).

... **a** Brought the Ark of the Covenant to Jerusalem

... **b** Tried to kill the man who became king after him

... **c** Was known for his wisdom

... **d** Spared the life of Israel's first king

... **e** Built the temple

... **f** Married a large number of foreign wives

... **g** Wrote two psalms about his response to God's conviction of sin in his life

... **h** Turned to witchcraft

1) Saul
2) David
3) Solomon

3 Suppose you were teaching a group of people that God forgives sin and continues to use the person who truly repents. The account of which king would provide the best illustration to use?
a) Saul
b) David
c) Solomon

4 Put the following ten events in this era of Israel's history in order. Write 1 in front of the event which occurred first, 2 in front of the event which occurred next, and so forth.

.... **a** Saul was anointed as king.

.... **b** David was anointed in Bethlehem.

.... **c** Solomon was born.

.... **d** The people asked Samuel for a king.

.... **e** Saul was rejected as king.

.... **f** David ruled Judah from Hebron.

.... **g** David built an altar on the threshing floor of Araunah.

.... **h** Solomon built a temple for the Lord.

.... **i** Absalom drove David from his throne for a time.

.... **j** David took the city of Jerusalem and became king of all Israel.

5 Match each of the following lessons or statements (left side) to the person with whom it is most closely associated (right side).

.... **a** His request for wisdom to rule God's people pleased the Lord.

.... **b** Though he knew the influence of God's Spirit, his disobedience to God finally caused him to be rejected as king.

.... **c** He continued to be faithful in praying for Israel though they had sinned.

.... **d** Because of the influence of his many foreign wives, he turned from the Lord and worshipped other gods.

.... **e** He had been anointed as king but spent many years waiting for God's time for him to actually become king.

1) Samuel
2) Saul
3) David
4) Solomon

answers to study questions

10 My answer: Because of his disobedience, Saul seemed to be depressed and in a state of spiritual darkness. The only time he felt relief was when David played his harp for him.

1 a) He was to be God's choice and an Israelite, not a foreigner.
   b) He was to have a copy of God's law made for himself. He was to keep this copy nearby, read from it, and obey it. He was to realize that he was subject to God like all the other Israelites.
   c) He was not to have a large number of horses or buy them from Egypt. He was not to have many wives or make himself rich. He was not to think of himself as better than the people.

11 Because he respected Saul as the one who had been chosen by God and anointed as king

2 Because in asking for a king they took themselves out from under God's direct authority and placed themselves under man's.

12 a) False
   b) False
   c) True

3 a) His main obligation was to know the law and obey it. If he did this, the result would be a long reign for him and for his descendants.
   b) He would take from the people to build up his royal household and army. As a result, the people would complain bitterly, but God would not hear them.

13 About 4 to 5 times larger

4 Samuel promised to continue to pray for them and teach them what was right for them to do.

14 a) He confessed his sin and asked God to make him clean. He humbled himself and repented.
   b) Your answer. David's attitude shows us how we should respond when God convicts us of sin.

A Kingdom United **165**

5 Your answer

15 a 3) Ruling over Judah
   b 2) Awaiting God's time
   c 4) Ruling over all Israel
   d 2) Awaiting God's time
   e 4) Ruling over all Israel
   f 1) Anointed as king
   g 2) Awaiting God's time
   h 3) Ruling over Judah
   i 4) Ruling over all Israel

6 God gave him a new nature.

16 Your answer could include the following (or other) similarities: 1) Both had an inner room in which the Ark of the Covenant rested; 2) Both had altars for sacrifice; and 3) Both were indwelt by the presence of the Lord. The main difference between them is that while the Tent was portable and had been moved from place to place during the time Israel wandered in the desert, the temple was not. It served as the permanent center of worship for the Israelites who had now been settled in their land.

7 Your chart should look similar to this:

Saul's Victories		Saul's Failures	
Reference	*Description*	*Reference*	*Description*
1 Samuel 14:1–23	Defeated the Philistines at Gibeah and saved the city of Jabesh	1 Samuel 13:8–13	Disobeyed God by acting as priest and offering sacrifices
1 Samuel 15:1–7	Defeated the Amalekites, fighting from Havilah to Shur	1 Samuel 15:8–23	Disobeyed God's command to completely destroy the Amalekites
1 Samuel 11:1–15	Defeated the Ammonites		

17 According to verses 7–8, God would abandon the temple and it would become a pile of ruins.

  8 a) did not think it was necessary for him to completely obey the Lord. (This is the real reason. Saul's acts of disobedience given in statements b) and c) came from his attitude of disrespect towards the Lord's will and commands.)

18 a) False
   b) True
   c) False

 9 a) They were both tall and handsome.
   b) Eliab was rejected because God saw his heart.
   c) God's choice indicated that David's heart was right with God.

19 c) In his first years as king . . . .

for your notes

LESSON 7: Writings of a Kingdom Age

The Old Testament includes five books known as poetry or wisdom literature. These are Job, Psalms, Proverbs, Ecclesiastes, and the Song of Songs. In contrast to the books we have already studied in this course, these books do not deal primarily with historical events. They deal, rather, with the experiences of life that were familiar to the Israelites. The problems, beliefs, attitudes, and emotions that are expressed in this literature give us insight into their lives.

While most of these writings were produced during the kingdom age, some of them were written earlier. Nevertheless, the experiences they deal with are common to people everywhere at every time of history. These writings speak to us today! The Holy Spirit has caused them to be preserved for our consideration, enjoyment, and growth.

As you study this lesson you will understand why these writings are beautiful in every language. You will discover the main theme and value of each one and learn why many Christians find them to be so meaningful and inspirational. Your spiritual and devotional life will be enriched as a result.

Writings of a Kingdom Age

lesson outline

The Writings and Their Form
Writings for Wisdom
Writings for Devotion

lesson objectives

When you finish this lesson you should be able to:

- Name the five books of wisdom and poetry.
- Identify the basic poetic styles found in the writings of wisdom and poetry.
- State the main teaching of the book of Job.
- Summarize the book of Proverbs.
- Identify the main message of the book of Ecclesiastes.
- Describe the book of Psalms.
- Distinguish between the literal and spiritual meanings of the Song of Songs.

learning activities

1. Read each of the books of poetry and wisdom in your Bible as directed by the lesson.
2. Study the lesson development according to the usual method. Answer each of the questions, review the lesson, and take the self-test. Be sure to check your answers with those given.

key words

allegorical	parallelism	synonymous
antithetic	philosophy	synthetic
interpretation	poem	translated
intimate	rhyme	wisdom

lesson development

THE WRITINGS AND THEIR FORM

The Writings

Objective 1. *Name the five books of wisdom and poetry.*

The books of the Bible which we will study in this lesson include those which many people regard as their favorites. Among the authors of these books were kings, prophets, poets, and common people. But though we are living in a time and culture different from theirs, the basic teachings of their writings are still valuable to us. These books show us that God relates to our lives in practical ways. He is concerned with our suffering, our business, our family life, and our desire to worship Him.

Application

1 The five books of poetry and wisdom are ....,............,............, and ....

2 The book of the Bible that comes immediately before Job is named................ The book of the Bible that immediately follows Song of Songs (or Song of Solomon) is

named ....

Their Form

Objective 2. *Identify the basic poetic styles found in the writings of wisdom and poetry.*

The books of wisdom and poetry are written in a poetic style called *parallelism*. This style is the main feature of Hebrew poetry. Parallelism means that the *thoughts* which are expressed are similar or balanced in some way (parallel). This style is in contrast to *rhyme,* in which the *sounds* of the words (usually the last word in each line) are similar. Notice this contrast below.

> Rhyme: Only one life, 'twill soon be past,
> Only what's done for Christ will last.
>
> Parallelism: You make springs flow in the valleys,
> And rivers run between the hills
> (Psalm 104:10).

Thus Hebrew poetry has great beauty, but this beauty comes primarily from the thoughts expressed. The wonderful thing about this style is that the beauty of the poetry is not lost when the poem is translated.

Application

3 The beauty of Hebrew poetry (parallelism) can be kept when the poetry is translated because it
a) lies in the balanced thoughts which can be put into other words.
b) has to do with special words which have the same sound and length.
c) can be found even if the meaning of the words cannot be understood.

There are three main kinds of parallelism:

1. *Synonymous*—the second line repeats the meaning of the first in different words.

2. *Synthetic*—the second line adds a new thought to the first (on the same theme or subject).

3. *Antithetic*—the second line gives a thought whose meaning is opposite to that of the first.

Application

4 Match each example of poetic style (left side) to the word which names it (right side).

... **a** Evil people are trapped in their own sin, While honest people are happy and free.

... **b** When I survey the wondrous cross, My richest gain I count but loss.

... **c** Evil does not grow in the soil, Nor does trouble grow out of the ground.

... **d** How hard it is to find a capable wife! She is worth far more than jewels!

... **e** He protects everyone who loves him, But he will destroy the wicked.

1) Rhyme
2) Synonymous
3) Synthetic
4) Antithetic

As you read these books of poetry and wisdom, try to recognize each of these different kinds of parallelism.

WRITINGS FOR WISDOM

Job—Dealing With Suffering

Read Job 1–15, 28–35, 38–42

Objective 3. *State the main teaching of the book of Job.*

It is likely that Job lived during the times of the patriarchs between Abraham and Moses. He is referred to in the book of Ezekiel along with Noah and Daniel (Ezekiel 14:14, 20). The book which bears his name is probably the oldest of the Bible books; it is also a poetic masterpiece. Its theme is human suffering—one of humanity's universal, unsolved problems.

The key word of the book is *test* or *trial*. Job spoke of God, "'When he has tested me, I will come forth as gold'" (Job 23:10). A simple outline of the book is as follows:

1. *Job 1:1–3:26.* Job and his three friends are introduced; Job has been reduced to poverty and misery.
2. *Job 4:1–31:40.* Job and his three friends discuss his suffering.
3. *Job 32:1–37:24.* Elihu speaks; he says that suffering is a means of purifying and chastening.
4. *Job 38:1–41:34.* God speaks; man cannot understand all the ways of the Creator, for His ways are above man's ways.
5. *Job 42:1–7.* Job worships God; his fortunes are restored to him in double measure.

In the book four basic views or ideas about suffering can be seen. We may call these views that of Satan, of the saint, of the sufferer, and of the Savior.

1. *Satan's view:* People serve God only for the riches and honor it brings (Job 1:1–2:8). He used this philosophy later when he tempted Jesus (Matthew 4:1–11).
2. *Friends' view:* (the view of Job's friends Eliphar, Bildad, and Zophar, who agree for the most part): The righteous are always rewarded and the sinner always suffers. Thus, they concluded, Job as a great sufferer must have been a great sinner (Job 4:7).
3. *Sufferer's view:* (the view of Elihu): Suffering is always the Father's discipline to bring us back to His purpose. Elihu's speeches are a far more just defense of God.
4. *Savior's view:* God revealed himself to Job. He teaches that the godly are allowed to suffer so that they might see themselves. Job, although a good man, was self-righteous.

The book of Job shows us that trials and suffering are not always for our punishment. Sometimes they are allowed to come into our lives so that we may be trained and educated. An athlete, for example, does not undergo strict discipline for punishment. His discipline prepares him to run the race. In the same way God is always preparing us for the work we each must do. And sometimes He does this through the discipline of trials and suffering. He has a wise purpose in it all. He wants to show us His wisdom.

Application

5 A person who had the "Savior's view" concerning suffering would say that when we suffer we
a) need to ask ourselves if we should continue to serve God.
b) find out that it is a result of our disobedience.
c) come to know ourselves and God in a new way.

6 Which of the following statements is the best description of the main teaching of the book of Job?
a) Man cannot understand the ways of God, so he must accept all the suffering he experiences as punishment for his sin.
b) Suffering is not always the result of sin, but godly people who experience it should respond to God in humility and worship.
c) People who serve God faithfully do not go through trials because God does not allow them to suffer.

Proverbs—Dealing With Life

Read Proverbs 1–10, 13–16, 29–31

Objective 4. *Summarize the book of Proverbs.*

The book of Proverbs is a marvelous collection of wise sayings. The Jews likened it to the outer court of the temple, the place where the Jew met other people. Proverbs is the godly man on his feet, for it seems to show us that godliness is practical. Every relationship is mentioned. In it we find our duty to God, our neighbor, our parents, our children, and even our country all mentioned.

The author of most of the book of Proverbs was Solomon. He was so wise that he was described as actually representing wisdom in himself (1 Kings 3:3–28; 4:29–30; 5:12). Many foreign rulers sought his advice (2 Chronicles 9:1–24). Along with Solomon (Proverbs 1:1, 10:1), the following additional authors are mentioned: a) The words of the wise (22:17); b) The Proverbs of Solomon copied by the men of Hezekiah (25:1); c) Agur (30:1); and d) King Lemuel (31:1). The book of Proverbs may be divided into three main sections:

1. Counsel for young men: chapters 1–10.

2. Counsel for all humankind: chapters 11–20.

3. Counsel for kings and rulers: chapters 21–31.

A notable part of this remarkable book is chapter 8. It is a forceful, beautiful description of wisdom. Many students of the Bible have noticed similarities between this chapter and certain descriptions of Jesus Christ which are found in the New Testament. In Colossians 2:3, for example, Christ is described as the One "in whom are hidden all the treasures of wisdom and knowledge." For a refreshing exercise, as you read verses of Proverbs, try putting the name *Christ* in place of the word *wisdom*.

Application

7 Compare Proverbs 8:23–31 with John 1:1–2 and Hebrews 1:2. In your notebook, name two things about wisdom (Proverbs 8:23–31) which are also true of Christ (John 1:1–2, Hebrews 1:2).

8 Read in your Bible the verses in Proverbs given in the references below (right side). Then match each one to the subject it deals with (left side).

....**a** Gossip

....**b** Idleness

....**c** Dishonesty

....**d** Humility

....**e** Guidance

....**f** Honesty

1) 3:5–6
2) 6:6–8
3) 11:1
4) 11:13
5) 16:18

9 The contents of all the book of Proverbs can best be summarized as
a) a group of wise sayings concerning our duty to God.
b) an explanation of how kings should behave.
c) practical wisdom applicable to all of life's relationships.

Ecclesiastes—Dealing With Despair

Read Ecclesiastes 1:1–12:14

Objective 5. *Identify the main message of the book of Ecclesiastes.*

Ecclesiastes is a statement of a human philosophy of life. It is like a record of all that the human mind can think and religion can offer. The arguments in the book are not God's arguments; they are God's record of humanity's arguments. Some of the arguments which are presented by man are in opposition to teaching found elsewhere in the Bible (see 1:15; 3:19; and 8:15).

The author identifies himself as "Solomon son of David, king of Israel" (1:1). Many believe that this book is a dramatic account of Solomon's own experience. The author asks a question: what is most valuable as a goal for life? He doubts that there really is an answer to this question. His experience shows that everything people seek after for satisfaction brings only despair. They seek satisfaction apart from God (1:1–3). They seek satisfaction in science (1:4–11). Philosophy does not give them an answer (1:12–18). Neither does pleasure (2:1–11) including happiness, drunkenness, work, possessions, wealth, and music. All are empty.

The author turns to materialism (2:12–26), an attitude of fatalism (3:1–15), and general but impersonal religion (3:16–22). These are also vain. It is not easy to please God (5:1–8), and riches bring no joy (5:9–16). Neither does being good (7:1–12).
Finally, he comes to an important conclusion: "Fear God and keep his commandments, for this is the whole duty of man" (12:13).

Application

10 What is the main message of the book of Ecclesiastes?
a) It gives us a record of Solomon's thoughts concerning riches and wealth.
b) It shows us that there is nothing worth doing.
c) It teaches us that everything eventually brings despair except obedience to God.
d) It points out that rich and poor men will all meet the same fate.

WRITINGS FOR DEVOTION

God created humans for fellowship with Him. As we have learned from the message of Ecclesiastes, humanity finds no meaning for life apart from fellowship with God. One of the main ways in which a believer has fellowship with God is through worship. When we worship God, we recognize His worth. We may be busy working for God, but only our true devotion and personal expression of worship to Him will bring lasting satisfaction. The two books of poetry we study in this section are both examples of and means for this experience.

Psalms—Praise and Prayer

Read Psalms 1–41, 79–91, 119–150

Objective 6. *Describe the book of Psalms.*

For more than 2,000 years the book of Psalms has been one of the most popular and best-loved books in the Old Testament. Beginning from the time of David, the Israelites used these songs in their worship of God. Christians today of every race and nation use them and sing from them. Their great popularity comes from the fact that they deal with the common experiences of the human race.

The title *Psalms* means "Praise" or the "Book of Praises." The Psalms magnify and praise the Lord. His names, His word, and His goodness are all honored.

About two-thirds of the Psalms name a specific author; among these are David (who wrote 73), Asaph (12), the sons of Korah (10), Solomon (2), and Moses (1). Ethan and Heman, two men compared for wisdom with Solomon (1 Kings 4:31), wrote one each.

But remember, Asaph was David's appointed choir master. The sons of Korah seem to have been a special group of singers from the Levites in David's day. Many of the Psalms that name no author seem to fall naturally to David. The shadow of David is everywhere in the Psalms. He shared his life openly with us, and his writings have given each of us an opportunity to know that God cares for us even in discouraging moments.

In the traditional collection, the 150 Psalms are divided into five units or "books." Each unit ends with a statement of praise. The five units are as follows: 1) Psalms 1–41; 2) Psalms 42–72; 3) Psalms 73–89; 4) Psalms 90–106; and 5) Psalms 107–150. Of course, each psalm is also a single unit in itself.

The Psalms can also be divided into groups according to their theme or subject. These groups include the following: Prayers of the righteous, songs of repentance and confession, songs of praise, songs about Israel's history, songs about the Messiah (Jesus), songs in distress, and songs of instruction.

Application

11 Read each of the Psalms listed below (left side) and match it to the group to which you believe it belongs (right side).

... **a** Psalm 1

... **b** Psalm 32

... **c** Psalm 105

... **d** Psalm 111

... **e** Psalm 142

... **f** Psalm 149

1) Repentance and confession
2) Instruction
3) History
4) Distress
5) Praise

The Psalms also contain many prophecies concerning Christ, the Messiah. Many of these were fulfilled in His first coming; others will be fulfilled when He comes again.

Application

12 Read in Psalms each of the verses listed in the references below. After each reference, write a word or two saying what it tells about Christ.

a) 2:8...

b) 22:16...

c) 110:4...

d) 118:22..

The Psalms show us an important principle we must all learn to follow in our relationship with God: honesty. Fellowship with God, like fellowship with a friend, demands truth. The attitude David showed in the Psalms gives us an example of what God expects from us in worship and prayer. God wants us to express our true feelings. Whether you are—like David was—in the temple of worship, the cave of hiding, the pit of despair, or the dance of joy, there is a psalm to express your feeling. Make the Psalms your personal book.

Application

13 Read 2 Samuel 11 and 12. Then read Psalm 51. What was David's response to the message of God's prophet?

....

14 What did David say in Psalm 5:3?

....

Do you have a definite time each day of devotion, praise, and prayer? If you do not, will you choose a time and begin now? It is very important!

Application

15 Circle the letter in front of each TRUE statement.
a) Although the Psalms were written long ago, they are used by Christians today.
b) About three-fourths of the Psalms were written by David.
c) The Psalms show us that discouragement and distress are not experienced by godly people.
d) The Psalms have prophecies concerning the death of Christ.
e) Some Psalms describe events in Israel's history.

Song of Songs—Loyalty and Love

Read Song of Songs 1:1–8:14

Objective 7. *Distinguish between the literal and spiritual meanings of the Song of Songs.*

This book is one of the 1005 songs written by Solomon (1 Kings 4:32). The title "Song of Songs" suggests that this was the best of all of them (in some Bibles it is called "Song of Solomon"). Because of its subject, many explanations have been given for its inclusion in the Bible. As we study these explanations, we will discover that this book has a special message for us.

In its literal or actual meaning, the song is about the warm emotions of human love and marriage. The main speakers are a country maiden called the girl of Shulam or the Shulammite (6:13), her lover, and a group of Jerusalem women. According to one interpretation, the country maiden has been taken to the royal court (1:1–2:7). Although the king expresses his love for her, she longs for her shepherd lover (2:8–7:9). At the end, she is reunited with him (7:10–8:14). Many other interpretations have also been given.

Writings of a Kingdom Age

The Jewish people saw the Song of Songs as a picture of the relationship between God and His people Israel. It was read each year at the Passover celebration. As the Israelites heard it, they were reminded of God's love for them in their deliverance from Egyptian slavery. The bond between Israel (the Shulammite maiden) and God (her shepherd lover) was so strong that no worldly appeal (the king) could break it. Other passages in the Old Testament also picture the relationship between Israel and God to be like that of a marriage (see Isaiah 50:1; Ezekiel 16, 23; and Jeremiah 3:1–20). This picture is also used in the New Testament, where the relationship between Christ and the church is described as a "marriage" (see Ephesians 5).

Application

16 Read each statement below concerning the Song of Songs (left side). Match it to the word which names the kind of meaning it portrays (right side).

... **a** The Shulammite maiden dreams of her shepherd lover.

... **b** God's love for Israel is beautiful and intimate.

... **c** The shepherd calls the maiden to come with him.

... **d** Israel is loyal to God who loves her.

... **e** The bond between Israel and God is very strong.

1) Literal
2) Spiritual

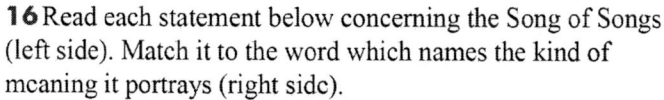

Like the Psalms, the Song of Songs is a call for the believer to enter into an intimate love relationship with God.

self-test

1 Following is the first line of a verse from Proverbs. Which would be the second line if the verse is one written in antithetical parallelism? A good man's words are like pure silver . . .

a) a wicked man's ideas are worthless.
b) they will benefit many people.
c) a righteous man's talk is a fountain of life.

2 Circle each TRUE statement about the book of Ecclesiastes.
a) It says that wealth is an unworthy goal in life.
b) It concludes that happiness comes only from obeying God.
c) David was its author.
d) Moses was its author
e) It teaches that hard work brings ultimate happiness.

3 The relationship between God and His people is spoken of in the New Testament as that of a "marriage" (Ephesians 5). In the Old Testament, a similar picture can be found in
a) Job.
b) Psalms.
c) Proverbs.
d) Ecclesiastes.
e) Song of Songs.

4 A person who understood the message of Job would say that Job suffered because God wanted to
a) make him stop leading a sinful and wicked life.
b) teach him new things about himself and God.
c) show him that all his friends understood God's purpose.
d) have Satan see that Job was being judged for his sin.

5 Suppose you wanted to lead a Bible study on ways to worship and praise the Lord. Which book would be the best to study?
a) Job
b) Psalms
c) Proverbs
d) Ecclesiastes

Writings of a Kingdom Age

6 The Jews likened the book of Proverbs to the outer court of the temple because it
a) explains the rules about offering different sacrifices.
b) has a section about the duties of the priests.
c) applies wisdom to human relationships.

7 The verses below are taken from each of the five books of poetry and wisdom. Match each one (left side) to the book to which you think it belongs (right side).

.... **a** Praise God with shouts of joy, all people! Sing to the glory of his name; offer him glorious praise!

.... **b** Have you asked God to show you your faults, and have you agreed to stop doing evil?

.... **c** I have seen everything done in this world, and I tell you, it is all useless. It is like chasing the wind.

.... **d** Let me hear your voice from the garden, my love; my companions are waiting to hear you speak.

.... **e** Then I knew only what others have told me, but now I have seen you with my own eyes.

.... **f** Do not try to talk sense to a fool; he cannot appreciate it.

1) Job
2) Proverbs
3) Ecclesiastes
4) Psalms
5) Song of Songs

answers to study questions

9 c) practical wisdom applicable to all of life's relationships.

1 Job, Psalms, Proverbs, Ecclesiastes, and Song of Songs.

10 c) It teaches us that everything eventually brings despair except obedience to God.

2 Esther, Isaiah

11 a 2) Instruction
  b 1) Repentance and confession
  c 3) History
  d 5) Praise
  e 4) Distress
  f 5) Praise

3 a) lies in the balanced thoughts which can be put into other words.

12 a 2:8; He rules over all the earth.
  b 22:16; His hands and feet were torn or pierced.
  c 110:4; He is a priest in the line of Melchizedek.
  d 118:22; He is the rejected stone which has become the most important one.

4 a 4) Antithetic
  b 1) Rhyme
  c 2) Synonymous
  d 3) Synthetic
  e 4) Antithetic

13 He confessed his sin and repented.

5 c) come to know ourselves and God in a new way.

14 He said that he prayed to the Lord in the morning.

6 b) Suffering is not always the result of sin, but godly people who experience it should respond to God in humility and worship.

15 a), d), and **e)** are true

7 Wisdom existed before creation and had a part in creation.

16 a 1) Literal
  b 2) Spiritual
  c 1) Literal
  d 2) Spiritual
  e 2) Spiritual

8 a 4) 11:13
  b 2) 6:6–8
  c 3) 11:1
  d 5) 16:18
  e 1) 3:5–6
  f 3) 11:1

LESSON 8: A Kingdom Divided

In Lesson 7 we paused in our study of the history of Israel to consider the writings of the kingdom age—the marvelous books of poetry and wisdom. Now we will return to the reign of king Solomon and follow the events of its last days and the years afterward.

Unlike the struggling tribes described in Judges, God's people in the days of the united kingdom were glorious. They subdued others. But during their days of blessing and prosperity they became careless. Idolatry increased, and they forgot the principle of success which Samuel had told them: "'Fear the Lord and serve him faithfully with all your heart'" (1 Samuel 12:24). Solomon turned aside to false gods, and the Lord brought judgment upon him.

Soon the old tribal jealousies appeared. The shadows of division and destruction loomed like a storm cloud, blocking the glory of Israel's achievements. And worse, the division brought dishonor on the Lord's name among the nations. But God did not abandon His people. As you study this era of their history you will become acquainted with the messages He gave them through His prophets. You will learn many lessons to apply to your own life today.

A Kingdom Divided

lesson outline

Division of the United Kingdom
Description of the Divided Kingdom
History of the Divided Kingdom

lesson objectives

When you finish this lesson you should be able to:

- State the causes and results of the division of the kingdom.
- Identify the characteristics and relationships of the northern and southern kingdoms.
- Describe the content of the books of Samuel, Kings, and Chronicles.
- Using a chart, list facts concerning the kings of Israel and Judah.
- Distinguish between prophetic messages predicting future events and prophetic messages giving principles of right and wrong that can be applied to life today.
- Match verses representing the themes of the prophetic books to the book to which they belong.

learning activities

1. Read in your Bible each section of Scripture as the lesson directs you to. This lesson has a large amount of Bible reading, so you may need to spend more time in order to complete it.
2. Study the lesson carefully.
3. When you have finished it, review Unit 2 (Lessons 5–7).
4. Complete the lesson. When you have reviewed Unit 2 (Lessons 5–7), complete Unit Student Report 2 and return Answer Sheet 2 to your national GU office if you live outside the United States or to your local church's CED learning center coordinator if you live in the United States.

(If you are currently incarcerated in a jail or prison in the United States you may mark your answers on the scantron answer sheet provided and send to the following address: CED, Global University, 1211 S. Glenstone Ave., Springfield, MO 65804.)

key words

allegiance	dynasty	remnant
assassination	genealogy	tribute
B.C.	political	writing prophet
current affairs	prediction	

A Kingdom Divided

lesson development

DIVISION OF THE UNITED KINGDOM

Read 1 Kings 11:14; 1 Chronicles 10–11

Objective 1. *State the causes and results of the division of the kingdom.*

God had warned His people through Moses, Joshua, and Samuel that sin would bring destruction. It was not an outside force which defeated them, but the fact that they themselves forsook God. They were not spared from God's judgment on their sin.

Solomon's Idolatry

God warned Solomon twice about worshipping foreign gods. Yet "Solomon did not keep the Lord's command" (1 Kings 11:10). For this reason the Lord told him the kingdom would be taken away from him, though not in his lifetime. God said that He would give one tribe to Solomon's son "'for the sake of David . . . and for the sake of Jerusalem'" (1 Kings 11:13).

The sin of Solomon and of the people in forsaking God and turning to abominable idolatry was the main reason why the kingdom was divided.

Application

1 Read 1 Kings 11:27–39 and answer the following questions in your notebook.
a) What reason did the prophet Ahijah give for the division of the kingdom?
b) How would the kingdom be divided?

Rehoboam's Attitude

A second reason for the division of the kingdom was the attitude of Solomon's son Rehoboam, who became king after

Solomon. The people had become restless under the heavy taxes and burdens of Solomon's latter days. They asked their new king to give them relief. But Rehoboam ignored the wise counsel of the elders and consulted his young friends. He answered after three days: "'My father made your yoke heavy; I will make it even heavier. My father scourged you with whips; I will scourge you with scorpions'" (1 Kings 12:14). Thereafter, the people rebelled and set up a northern kingdom under Jeroboam, a former official in Solomon's government.

Tribal Jealousy

A third reason for the division was the ancient jealousy between the tribe of Judah and the great tribe of Ephraim to the north. You will remember that Joshua had been an Ephraimite. Saul, on the other hand, was chosen from the tribe of Benjamin and David from the tribe of Judah. The sharp rivalry between Judah and Ephraim is seen in the biblical account. While they obeyed God there was unity. But when they did not the division seemed unavoidable.

When the kingdom was divided into two rival states, the entire political structure collapsed. The Philistines, Syrians, Ammonites, and Moabites—nations whom Israel had subdued—regained their freedom. The economic disturbance was serious. These nations no longer paid tribute, and it was impossible for the divided tribes to keep control of the major trade routes. A great kingdom literally fell apart overnight, leaving two weak, second-rate powers.

Application

2 Read 1 Kings 12. When Rehoboam assembled an army to attack the tribes under Jeroboam, God told him to
a) go ahead and fight the rebellious tribes in order to keep unity.
b) wait until he received further instructions from the prophet.
c) send all the people home because the division was His will.

3 Read each statement about the division of the kingdom (left side). Then decide whether the statement gives a cause of (1) or a result of (2) the division and write the correct number in front of it.

... **a**	Rehoboam followed the advice of his younger friends.	1) Cause
... **b**	The nations Israel had subdued no longer paid tribute.	2) Result
... **c**	The control over the trade route was lost.	
... **d**	Both the people and the king turned away from worshipping the Lord.	
... **e**	Another kingdom was set up under Jeroboam, one of Solomon's former officials.	

DESCRIPTION OF THE DIVIDED KINGDOM

Objective 2. *Identify the characteristics and relationships of the northern and southern kingdoms.*

Their Names

We have seen that up to this time the name "Israel" has been used to refer to Jacob himself and all of his descendants (Genesis 32:22–32; 49:2; Joshua 1:2). After the kingdom was divided, however, the Bible uses "Israel" to refer to the northern kingdom of ten tribes whose first ruler was Jeroboam. At times the northern kingdom is also called "Ephraim," the name of its most influential tribe.

On the other hand, the southern kingdom of the tribes of Judah and Benjamin is called "Judah." It is important to keep these facts in mind when reading the different books of the Old Testament.

Their Contrasts

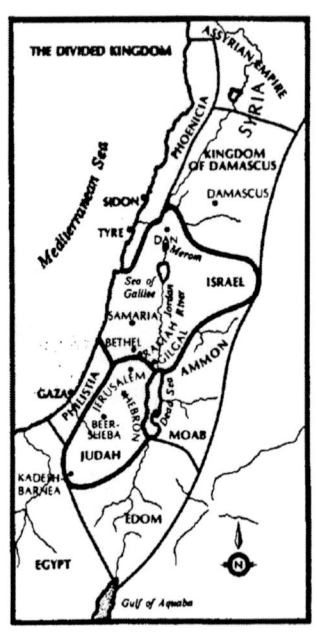

The northern kingdom (Israel) had many advantages over the southern kingdom (Judah). It possessed ten strong tribes whereas the southern kingdom had only two. (Sometimes, however, Judah and Benjamin are counted as one tribe.) As you will see by looking at this map of the two kingdoms, the northern one had a much larger area. It also had the best farming land—the fertile Jordan valley. Its population outnumbered that of Judah by three to one. In addition, the major military centers built by Solomon and David were there. So were the schools of the prophets in Bethel, Gilgal, and Ramah. The reasons for its existence was that God had allowed the kingdom to be divided in this way in judgment because of the people's sins.

But the southern kingdom, though smaller in land and population, possessed Jerusalem, the political and religious center of the nation. It was fear of the influence of Jerusalem which caused Jeroboam, the first king of the northern kingdom, to make a fatal error. This act brought God's immediate wrath and judgment upon him.

Application

4 Read 1 Kings 12:25–31. What did Jeroboam do to try to keep his people from going to worship in Jerusalem?

. . . .

After this act by Jeroboam, the priests, Levites, and many others from each tribe who were strong in loyalty to the Lord forsook the northern kingdom and transferred their allegiance to Judah. Judah was greatly strengthened by their addition. This meant that remnants of all the tribes were then found within Judah's borders (2 Chronicles 11:13-17).

The southern kingdom enjoyed one even greater advantage. It had only one family of kings, all from the descendants of David. God kept His promise to David, His servant! In contrast, the northern kingdom had nine separate dynasties or families of kings with nineteen wicked rulers. These dynasties followed one another by assassination, bloodshed, and revolution. Perhaps for this reason the southern kingdom outlasted the northern kingdom by 130 years. Below is a chart which summarizes the differences between these two kingdoms and a diagram which shows the length of time each one lasted.

ISRAEL	JUDAH
Northern, ten tribes Capital at Shechem, then Samaria Idol worship at Dan and Bethel	Southern, two tribes Capital at Jerusalem Worship in Temple at Jerusalem
Nine different dynasties All kings were bad Nineteen kings Lasted about 240 years	One ruling family Good and bad kings Nineteen kings, one queen Lasted 395 years
Kingdom fell in 722 B.C. Taken captive by Shalmanezer to Assyria	Kingdom fell in 586 B.C. Taken captive by Nebuchadnezzar to Babylon

```
                        Israel         722 B.C.
                       ┌────────────────to Assyria
  United Kingdom       │
  David—Solomon        │
                       │Judah          586 B.C.
                       └────────────────to Babylon
```

Application

5 According to the diagram and charts just given, the northern kingdom
a) was ruled by David.
b) had two religious centers.
c) lasted less time than the southern.

Their Relationship

You are aware of what civil war does in a nation. It leaves families divided. It leaves business, transportation, and social life destroyed. Israel had been one family, one language, and one nation. Now they were, as Ahijah had prophesied, like a garment torn into twelve pieces; ten pieces now united against two. The relationship between the two kingdoms went through four clearly-marked periods:

1. Mutual hostility. During this time the kings of Judah continued to try to regain authority over the ten tribes of the northern kingdom. There were about 60 years of constant warfare.

2. Close ties against a mutual enemy. Syria threatened the two kingdoms. King Ahab of Israel tried to form an alliance with Jehoshaphat, king of Judah, through the intermarriage of the royal families. The purpose was to unite against the increasing powers of Syria.

3. A period of fresh mutual hostility. When Jehu came to the throne in the northern kingdom he killed all the remaining people of the family of Ahab. This shattered the alliance which had been made by Ahab with the southern kingdom. The wound was never healed. The northern kingdom fell more and more into idolatry. There were a number of prophetic warnings, but the northern kingdom was finally carried away into captivity by the Assyrians in 722 B.C.

4. The southern kingdom alone. Assyria, Egypt, and finally the Chaldeans came to try to conquer Judah. The struggle went

A Kingdom Divided

on for about 130 years until 586 B.C. when Judah was taken into captivity by the Babylonians under Nebuchadnezzar.

Application

6 Match each fact (left side) to the kingdom which it describes (right side).

... **a** Possessed the best farming land

... **b** Had a smaller land area

... **c** Fell to Assyria in 722 B.C.

... **d** Was ruled by Jehu

... **e** Fell to Babylonia in 586 B.C.

... **f** Responsible for killing Ahab's family

... **g** Tried to regain control over the ten tribes

... **h** Had nine ruling dynasties

... **i** Had one ruling family

... **j** Jerusalem was its capital

... **k** Formed an alliance through marriage with the family of Jehoshaphat

1) Northern
2) Southern

HISTORY OF THE DIVIDED KINGDOM

The Records

Read 1 Kings 15–16, 20–22; 1 Chronicles 13:17; 28–29; 2 Chronicles 13–20

Objective 3. *Describe the content of the books of Samuel, Kings, and Chronicles.*

The history of the united and divided kingdom is recorded in the books of Samuel, Kings, and Chronicles. Together these books make up about one-fifth (20%) of the Old Testament. It is important to remember that this history is written from God's point of view.

For example, consider one of the kings of the northern kingdom named Omri. His family reigned for 44 years, the second longest dynasty of all of Israel. We learn from non-biblical records that Omri founded the most powerful ruling family in the northern kingdom. He moved the capital to Samaria, where he began a great city, and he regained territory from the Moabites. In fact, the Assyrians, who later conquered the northern kingdom, called it the land of Omri. Yet the Bible gives the actual events of Omri's reign in only two verses—1 Kings 16:23–24! It is important to keep this point of view in mind when studying these historical records.

Application

7 Read 1 Samuel 16:7 and 1 Kings 16:21–28. Why do you think so little is said about what Omri accomplished?

....

These books differ from each other regarding the importance they place on different aspects of the history they deal with. Let us consider the emphasis of each one.

1. The books of 1 and 2 Samuel show us the principles upon which God wanted the kingdom to be established. It was to be founded on the spiritual values taught by Samuel and ruled by kings who followed the example of David's submissive leadership.

2. The books of 1 and 2 Kings describe how the kingdom actually developed. We see how the prophecy given by Nathan to David (2 Samuel 7:12–16) was fulfilled. This prophecy said that David would always have descendants. First and Second Kings tell about both the northern and southern kingdom. They give much attention to the prophets such as Elijah and Elisha.

3. The books of 1 and 2 Chronicles emphasize the temple: its ceremonies of worship and official figures. With the priesthood and the temple as their main theme, these books

recount the history of the united kingdom under Saul, David, and Solomon. Then they deal mainly with the history of Judah, the southern kingdom. The northern kingdom of Israel is mentioned only when its events are related to those in the southern.

Following are two illustrations. The first shows the time span covered by these books. The second shows the differences in the themes of Kings and Chronicles.

THE BOOKS OF SAMUEL, KING, CHRONICLES

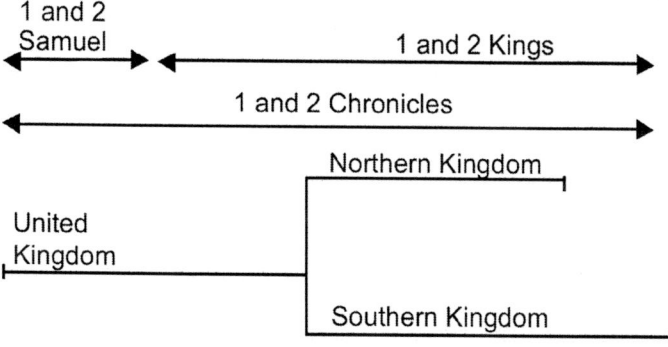

Kings	Chronicles
History of both Israel and Judah	History mainly of Judah
Emphasizes the prophets	Emphasizes the priests
Deals with the kingdom and the kings	Deals with the temple and the priests
Ends when the people go into captivity	Ends when the people come back out of captivity

Application

8 Circle the letter of each TRUE statement.
a) Kings and Chronicles both record the history of Judah.
b) Chronicles deals mainly with the lives of the prophets.
c) Kings emphasizes the history of the northern kingdom and its priests.
d) The books of Chronicles cover about the same time span as the books of Samuel and Kings together.
e) Chronicles ends when the people go into captivity.
f) The prophecy concerning David's kingdom is found in 2 Samuel.
g) Both Samuel and Kings deal with the reign of Saul.

The Kings

Read 2 Kings 20–24; 2 Chronicles 29–35

Objective 4. *Using a chart, list facts concerning the kings of Israel and Judah.*

The character of Israel and Judah, in one sense, was seen in their kings, because the role of the king in the spiritual destiny of the nation was crucial. What the king was, the people eventually became. This was true both for the good, or, as was usually the case, for the bad.

After Solomon the story of kings gives a sad picture of decline and backsliding. In the northern kingdom Jeroboam had set up the worship of golden bulls. As the first king, his example corrupted the nation and ultimately led to its destruction (1 Kings 16:7; 22:52; 2 Kings 10:31). In the southern kingdom Rehoboam permitted the Israelites to build places in which to worship false gods. They followed the wicked practices of the people that God had ordered them to drive out of Palestine (1 Kings 14:22–24).

But though most of the kings were bad, there were some that were good. The reign of Hezekiah in Judah, for example, was a wonderful time of faith and glory (2 Kings 18:1–20:21).

A Kingdom Divided

In the appendix at the end of this book you will find a chart entitled "Kings and Prophets of the Divided Kingdom." This chart gives the following information about each of the kings of Israel and Judah:

1. The year the king came to power, his name, and the Bible references telling where information concerning his reign is recorded. In the northern kingdom, kings who began dynasties are printed like this: JEROBOAM. The names of some of the kings are the same. This is because the royal families of both kingdoms intermarried and used the same names.

2. How the king gained his throne (by inheritance, assassination, or other means) and about how long he ruled. In some cases, two kings reigned at the same time, so the years do not always add up exactly.

3. A short description of his spiritual character.

4. The names of any prophets who were active during his reign. Prophets who have a book in the Bible by their name are printed in full capitalization; they are also called "writing prophets." Some prophets, like Amos, had a ministry in both kingdoms.

Now turn to the chart and find the name BAASHA in the list of the northern kingdom. As you will notice, the chart tells us: a) that Baasha came to power in the year 909, b) that he began a dynasty, c) that information about his reign is found in 1 Kings 15:32–16:7, d) that he gained his throne by assassination, e) that he ruled for 24 years, f) that he was a bad king, and g) that Jehu prophesied during the reign. (Remember that the years numbered before Christ count backwards, or become smaller, until the time of Christ which is numbered 0. The years before Christ are usually marked with the letters "B.C." meaning "before Christ." All the years in this chart are B.C.)

Application

9 In your notebook, answer the following questions by using the information given in the chart.
a) What was the name of king Jehoshaphat's son (he married Athaliah, the daughter of king Ahab of Israel)?
b) Now, what was the name of the next king of Judah, the son of Jehoram and Ahab's daughter Athaliah?
c) Who succeeded king Ahab in the northern kingdom?
d) To which dynasty did Jeroboam 2 belong?
e) Who came to power in Judah in 750?
f) Which kings of the southern kingdom might be considered very good? Where in the Bible would you read about them?
g) Which prophet was active at both the fall of Samaria and the reign of Hezekiah of Judah? Is there a book in the Bible by his name?
h) How many kings of the northern kingdom gained their power by assassination?
i) How long did king Amaziah of Judah reign?

You may want to study the lives of each of these kings in greater detail. If so, use the chart to help you in your study. The evil ways of the kings and the people ultimately brought destruction to both kingdoms. The northern kingdom fell in 722 B.C. and the southern in 586 B.C. God had foretold this 800 years earlier through Moses. Captivity and brokenness became the payment for rebellion and idolatry.

Application

10 Read Deuteronomy 28:33, 36. In your notebook, write what God said would happen if His people disobeyed Him.

The Prophets

Their Message; Read 1 Kings 17–19; 2 Kings 1–8, 19–20

Objective 5. *Distinguish between prophetic messages predicting future events and prophetic messages giving principles of right and wrong that can be applied to life today.*

During the dark days of the northern and southern kingdoms God raised up many prophets to warn His people. Of these, twelve have books by their names in the Old Testament. As prophets, their messages were not only about the events of the future but also about God's will for the present. They often had insight into the current affairs of their nation. In 2 Kings 17:13 we read that God sent His prophets to warn Israel and Judah: "'Turn from your evil ways. Observe my commands and decrees, in accordance with the entire Law that I commanded your fathers to obey and that I delivered to you through my servants the prophets.'" These men were fearless in speaking to kings and people alike about their sins and the coming judgment.

The prophet was a specially-chosen man. He did not inherit his position as did the king or priest. God's choice of him was not influenced by his family, tribe, or intellectual training. The prophet had two major responsibilities. He was called upon to 1) receive something from God and to 2) produce or speak on behalf of God. The prophet's message thus came from God, not from his own thoughts. Only the false prophets announced what they thought. As God's messenger speaking on His behalf, the prophet was to fearlessly bring God's word to the people.

Application

11 Look again at the chart of the divided kingdom in the back of this study guide. In your notebook, write the name of each prophet during this time who has a book by his name in the Bible.

The prophet's message was received and given out under God's inspiration. But at the same time his own mental ability, personality, and way of speaking were not lost. He was an instrument in God's hand, not a machine. This is a most important distinction, for the results of God's inspiration were in no way like the results of the influence of evil spirits who actually control people.

The source of the prophet's message was important, and so was the message itself. The message of the prophets had three parts:

1. A message to *their own age* or generation directly from God.

2. A message of *predicted future events* such as the following: a) the failure of God's chosen people and God's judgment on them and the nations around them; b) the coming of the Messiah and His rejection and final glory; and c) the establishment of the Messiah's kingdom here on earth.

3. A living message to *us who live today* containing principles of right and wrong.

The message the prophet gave to his own generation was often a combination of predictions of future events and principles of right and wrong. We can learn much from these messages, both about the Messiah and His kingdom and about the principles of right and wrong which we can apply to our lives today. Habakkuk 1:6, for example, is a prediction of a future event, whereas 2:4 and 2:18 contain principles of right and wrong. Take a moment now to read and consider the meaning of these verses of Scripture.

Application

12 Read the following verses from the book of Micah (left side). Write 1 in front of each one which represents a definite prophecy about the future and 2 in front of each one which gives principles of right and wrong that we can follow today.

... **a** Micah 1:6–7
... **b** Micah 2:1–3
... **c** Micah 3:8–11
... **d** Micah 5:2
... **e** Micah 6:6–8

1) Future events
2) Principles of right and wrong

Their Ministries

Objective 6. *Match verses representing the themes of the prophetic books to the book to which they belong.*

To the Northern Kingdom

The writing prophets to the northern kingdom during the time before the Assyrian captivity in 722 B.C. were Jonah, Amos, and Micah. In addition, the northern kingdom was ministered to by Elijah, Elisha, Ahijah, Jehu, Micaiah, and Oded. Each prophet had a special ministry given to him by the Lord. Elijah and Elisha, for example, performed many miracles (see 1 Kings 17 and 2 Kings 4). Jonah was sent to a foreign city, Nineveh, to warn its people of the coming judgment. Read Jonah 1–4 before continuing. Make a check mark here when you have completed your reading: ☐

Application

13 Read each Scripture given below. Then in your notebook, write it down and next to it give the name of the prophet it tells about and a short description of what he did.
a) 1 Kings 14:1–17
b) 1 Kings 16:1–7

c) 1 Kings 18:20–39
d) 2 Kings 5:9–16
e) 2 Chronicles 28:9–11

The following is a brief summary of the messages God gave the northern kingdom through the writing prophets. Each would be a wonderful subject for you to study on your own.

Hosea: Hosea's love for and restoration of his own sinful, adulterous wife was a picture of God's forgiving love for sinful Israel. Chapters 1–3 are the account of Hosea's personal experience which are like God's dealings with spiritually adulterous Israel. Chapters 4–14 are the same message given in greater detail. Read Hosea 1–14 before continuing. Make a check mark here when you have completed your reading: ☐

Amos: Amos preached that a nation is responsible for its national sins. The heathen nations surrounding God's people were condemned to experience judgment for their national sins. Israel, however, received a more severe condemnation for its sins since Israel had greater light. Read Amos 1–9 before continuing. Make a check mark here when you have completed your reading: ☐

Micah: Micah preached to both the northern and southern kingdoms regarding the coming judgment and future restoration and blessing. Chapters 1–3 show a dark picture, chapters 4–5 a bright one, and chapter 6 more judgment. Then from 7:7 on, the book gives a glorious picture of Israel's future. Read Micah 1–7 before continuing. Make a check mark here when you have completed your reading: ☐

Application

14 Read the Scriptures about each of the prophets given below (right side). Then match each prophet to the sentence which tells about his message or activities (left side).

... **a** Successfully challenged the prophets of Baal

... **b** Said Judah would be attacked by Shishak of Egypt

... **c** Correctly identified the disguised wife of Jeroboam

... **d** Told Josiah that he would not see God's judgment on Jerusalem

1) Ahijah, 1 Kings 14:1–18
2) Huldah, 2 Kings 22:12–20
3) Shemaiah, 2 Chronicles 12:5–8
4) Elijah, 1 Kings 18:20–39

To the Southern Kingdom

The writing prophets to the southern kingdom during this time were Obadiah, Joel, Isaiah, Micah, Nahum, Habakkuk, Zephaniah, and Jeremiah. In addition, Shemaiah, Iddo, Azariah, Hanani, Eliezer, and Huldah gave God's messages to the people. Following is a brief summary of the messages of the writing prophets.

Joel: The country had been threatened with destruction because of devastating swarms of locusts and excessive drought. Though the plague was removed through fasting and prayer, Joel's prophecy used it as a picture of the terrible day of final judgment for all nations. The faithful will be rewarded while evil doers will be punished. Read Joel 1–3 before continuing. Make a check mark here when you have completed your reading: ☐

Isaiah: Isaiah was a nobleman and prophet of king Hezekiah's day who warned, comforted, and advised his rulers. He prophesied the captivity of Judah's kingdom but foretold the dawn of the new kingdom. He prophesied both the sufferings and the glory of the coming Messiah. Read Isaiah 1, 6–7, 39–44, 52–66 before continuing. Make a check mark here when you have completed your reading: ☐

Micah: Micah prophesied to both kingdoms. Review his message in the previous section.

Application

15 Compare Isaiah 43:5–7 with Micah 4:6–7. In both of these prophecies, God said that He would
a) scatter Israel among the nations.
b) gather His people from the nations.
c) judge His people and punish them.

Nahum: The foreign nation of Assyria was the subject of Nahum's prophecy. Assyria had oppressed Judah for a century: the doom of Nineveh, Assyria's capital, was pronounced, explained, and described by Nahum. Read Nahum 1–3 before continuing. Make a check mark here when you have completed your reading: ☐

Zephaniah: The "Day of the Lord" was stressed by Zephaniah. This day brings destruction to the false remnant who worship Baal (Chapter 1), and it brings purification and blessing to the true remnant of God's people. Read Zephaniah 1–3 before continuing. Make a check mark here when you have completed your reading: ☐

Jeremiah: Many have named him "the weeping prophet." He was from a priestly family. While still a boy he was called to be a prophet. For his loyalty to the preaching of God's word for half a century he was despised, feared, hated, and persecuted. Because he predicted the overthrow of Jerusalem and seventy years of captivity he was called a traitor and suffered much cruel treatment. Read Jeremiah 1–9, 18–19, 36–39, 52 before continuing. Make a check mark here when you have completed your reading: ☐

Lamentations: This book records Jeremiah's poetic expression of his grief at the destruction and desolation of

Jerusalem and the temple and at the captivity and miseries of the people. Read Lamentations 1–5 before continuing. Make a check mark here when you have completed your reading: ☐

Habakkuk: Habakkuk's message was that right would win. Judah was being punished by the wicked Babylonians, but the Babylonians would in turn be punished. Read Habakkuk 1–3 before continuing. Make a check mark here when you have completed your reading: ☐

Obadiah: The land of Edom would be judged for its mistreatment of God's people. Israel would be blessed. Read Obadiah 1 before continuing. Make a check mark here when you have completed your reading: ☐

Application

16 Match each verse (left side) to the name of the prophetic book (right side) to which it belongs.

... **a** You must love her just as I still love the people of Israel, even though they turn to other gods.

... **b** An army of locusts has attacked our land; they are powerful and too many to count.

... **c** But because of our sins he was wounded, beaten because of the evil we did.

... **d** The city of Zion [Jerusalem] is beautiful, but it will be destroyed.

... **e** His royal power will continue to grow; his kingdom will always be at peace.

1) Isaiah
2) Jeremiah
3) Hosea
4) Joel

Our study of the divided kingdom has helped us to see the decline of God's people. Finally, as the prophets had warned, first Israel and then Judah collapsed and were led into captivity. Yet, God revealed through the prophets a glorious future when the Prince of Peace will rule (Isaiah 9:6–7) and the nations will seek the Lord (Micah 4:2).

self-test

1 Which statement best describes the reason why the kingdom was divided?
a) The prophet Ahijah prophesied that ten tribes would be given to Jeroboam.
b) The people had been severely taxed by Solomon.
c) Solomon turned away from God to worship idols.

2 Circle the letter of each TRUE statement.
a) The northern kingdom had more land than the southern.
b) Ephraim was another name for the southern kingdom.
c) The southern kingdom possessed centers of worship at Dan and Bethel.
d) The name Israel was used to refer to the northern kingdom.
e) Once they were divided, the two kingdoms never formed any alliances.

3 Circle the letter in front of each correct completion. The books of 1 and 2 Kings
a) describe the reign of Solomon.
b) give most of their attention to the priests and the temple.
c) follow the books of 1 and 2 Chronicles in order in the Bible.
d) record the ministry of Elijah and Elisha.
e) cover a time span not included by 1 and 2 Chronicles.

4 Match each statement (left side) to the kingdom whose history it most closely describes (right side).

.... **a** This kingdom has a series of rulers among whom were both good and bad kings. It fell in 586 B.C. and the people were taken captive to Babylon.

.... **b** This kingdom's first ruler was Jeroboam, who set up idols for the people to worship. The prophet Elijah had a ministry to this kingdom during the reign of king Ahab.

.... **c** Six of the rulers of this kingdom obtained the throne by assassination. It was ruled by nine different dynasties.

1) Northern
2) Southern

5 What is the best explanation for the fact that both the southern and northern kingdoms eventually fell?
a) The prophets announced that God would bring judgment upon those who disobeyed Him.
b) The surrounding nations became stronger and were able to conquer Israel and Judah.
c) The people and most of the kings did not faithfully follow God.

6 Circle the letter in front of each TRUE statement about the prophets of the divided kingdom and their message.
a) Since the prophets' main messages concerned the future of Israel and Judah, they are of no interest to us today.
b) In some prophecies, natural events were used as an illustration of what would take place in the future.
c) Because the prophets were called by God to minister to His people, none of them were given messages for foreign nations.
d) One of the prophet's two main responsibilities was to choose the person who became the next king.
e) A prophet's message often contained principles of right and wrong that we can apply to our lives today.

> Before you continue your study with Lesson 9, be sure to complete your student report for Unit 2 and return Answer Sheet 2 to your instructor.

answers to study questions

9 a) Jehoram
  b) Ahaziah
  c) Ahaziah (this is an example of how the same names were used.)
  d) Jehu
  e) Jotham
  f) Hezekiah (2 Kings 18:1–20:21) and Josiah (2 Kings 22:1–23:30 and 2 Chronicles 34:1–35:27).
  g) Micah, yes
  h) Six
  i) 29 years

1 a) Solomon's rejection of the Lord, his worship of other gods, and his disobedience of the Lord's commands (or a similar answer).
  b) Ten tribes would be given to Jeroboam; one would remain with Solomon's son (Judah and Benjamin were counted as one).

10 He said that a foreign nation would take their crops and oppress them. They and their king would be taken captive to a foreign land and serve idols.

2 c) send all the people home because the division was His will.

11 Zechariah, Joel, Amos, Isaiah, Micah, Jeremiah, Zephaniah, Nahum, Habakkuk, Obadiah, Jonah, and Hosea (in any order).

3 a 1) Cause
  b 2) Result
  c 2) Result
  d 1) Cause
  e 2) Result

12 a 1) Future events
  b 2) Principles of right and wrong
  c 2) Principles of right and wrong
  d 1) Future events
  e 2) Principles of right and wrong

A Kingdom Divided

4 He set up two golden bulls, one at Dan and one at Bethel for the people to worship (or a similar answer).

13 a) Ahijah; he gave a message to Jeroboam's wife that her son would die. Later the son died.
  b) Jehu; he gave a message of judgment to Baasha that he and his family would be destroyed because of his sin.
  c) Elijah; he built an altar to God and prayed for God to send fire down from heaven. God answered his prayer.
  d) Elisha; he told Naaman to wash in the Jordan to be healed. Naaman obeyed and was healed.
  e) Oded; he rebuked the northern army for taking prisoners from Jerusalem and Judah.
(Your answers should be similar to these.)

5 b) had two religious centers.
  c) lasted less time than the southern.

14 a 4) Elijah, 1 Kings 18:20–39.
  b 3) Shemaiah, 2 Chronicles 12:5–8.
  c 1) Ahijah, 1 Kings 14:1–18
  d 2) Huldah, 2 Kings 22:12–20.

6 a 1) Northern   **g** 2) Southern
  b 2) Southern   **h** 1) Northern
  c 1) Northern   **i** 2) Southern
  d 1) Northern   **j** 2) Southern
  e 2) Southern   **k** 1) Northern
  f 1) Northern

15 b) gather His people from the nations.

7 Because according to God's point of view it is a person's spiritual character that is important, not his outward gain or accomplishments (or a similar answer).

16 a) 3) Hosea 3:1
  b) 4) Joel 1:6
  c) 1) Isaiah 53:5
  d) 2) Jeremiah 6:2
  e) 1) Isaiah 9:7

8 a) True
  b) False
  c) False
  d) True
  e) False
  f) True
  g) False

for your notes

Destruction and Rebuilding

Lessons
 9 Judgment and Captivity
10 Return and Restoration

LESSON 9
Judgment and Captivity

We have studied the purpose of God as it has been shown in the history of His people. From a small beginning—one man of faith—they had grown into a powerful nation. But then, they had become a divided house. Now we study a series of disasters which God allowed to come upon them because of their sins. Both kingdoms fell, and the captives spent many years in a foreign land.

The captivity of His people brought great sorrow to the heart of God. Nevertheless, the Bible teaches us that the Lord corrects everyone He loves, "'and he punishes everyone he accepts as a son'" (Hebrews 12:6). If God must ever deal with us in a drastic manner to turn us away from sin, He does so with a heart of love. In love God must often draw those who wander away back into fellowship with himself through severe trial.

As you study this period in the history of God's people, you will discover some of the lessons they learned through their bitter experiences. Some of these lessons brought them lasting spiritual benefits. And you will find in them truths that you can apply to your own life.

Judgment and Captivity **217**

lesson outline

The Rod of Judgment

The Experience of Captivity

lesson objectives

When you finish this lesson you should be able to:

- List in order the events before and during the fall of the northern and southern kingdoms.

- Give details on the captivity, the leaders that God raised up during it, and the lessons God's people learned from it.

learning activities

1. Study the lesson development; answer the study question. and complete the self-test as you have done in previous lessons. Read from the Bible as you are directed to by the lesson and study questions.

2. Pay close attention to the maps given in the lesson and be sure you understand them.

key words

Assyria	intervention	synagogue
Babylon	siege	vassal
exile	supremacy	

lesson development

THE ROD OF JUDGMENT

Objective 1. List in order the events before and during the fall of the northern and southern kingdoms.

We have become familiar with the warnings God gave to His people through the prophets. These warnings said that unfaithfulness to God had one result: disaster. God is patient, and judgment may be postponed, but ultimately unrighteousness would be judged. The Lord had tried to save His people, but they would not listen. Sometimes they responded with outward reforms, but there was no change in their inward life. Let us study the dark events of these years, however, in the light of one important understanding of the purpose God continued to have: He judged and purified His people, but He did not destroy them.

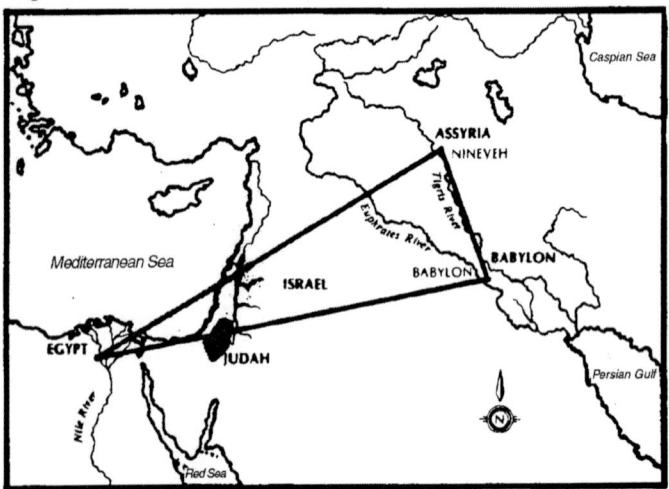

The Fall of the Northern Kingdom

We have seen how the nation of Israel was surrounded by three great powers: Egypt, Babylon, and Assyria. Each of these was trying to become the world's most powerful nation. Notice

Judgment and Captivity

the location of these nations in the preceding map. Israel and Judah were located in the middle of this triangle. When the people of God walked by faith, He protected them from these political pressures. But when they forsook Him, God used these nations first to warn, and finally to bring judgment upon them.

Application

1 Refer to the preceding map. Circle the letter in front of each TRUE statement.
a) Assyria is northwest of Judah and northeast of Babylon.
b) Israel and Judah are located at about the same distance from both Assyria and Babylon.
c) Egypt is closer to Assyria than to Judah and Israel.

During the 16th year of the reign of king Ahab of Israel, a great king came to the throne of Assyria. This was Shalmaneser III. He frequently came into contact with the borders of Israel because he was building a great empire. Before his death, the gains he made were lost because of conflict within Assyria itself. However, the rulers who followed him—Tiglath-pileser III, Shalmaneser V, and Sargon II—made Assyria the most important military and economic power in the area. This took them only 40 years. Ultimately, Israel was made a vassal state, paying tribute to Assyria for its existence. The prophets Amos, Hosea, and Isaiah had warned that this would happen. But Israel had continued in sin.

Application

2 Read 2 Kings 17:1–18. In your notebook, write the reasons why judgment came upon the northern kingdom.

The northern kingdom was not only guilty of the list of sins with which God had charged them, but also of rejecting the messages of the prophets. The nation could have been saved if it had listened. God's warnings to and patience with them should have produced righteousness. But finally, their repeated sin and rebellion brought judgment.

Because there was no genuine repentance, and because of the pride of Israel's leaders, God allowed Assyria to defeat them. Assyria laid a three-year siege to Samaria, the capital city of the northern kingdom. Then in 722 B.C. Sargon II captured the city and took the inhabitants of the northern kingdom into captivity. He resettled other captive tribes in the place where God's people had been (2 Kings 17:24). The descendants of these tribes are the Samaritans we read about in the Bible, such as in John 4. Notice on the following map where the captives of Israel were taken.

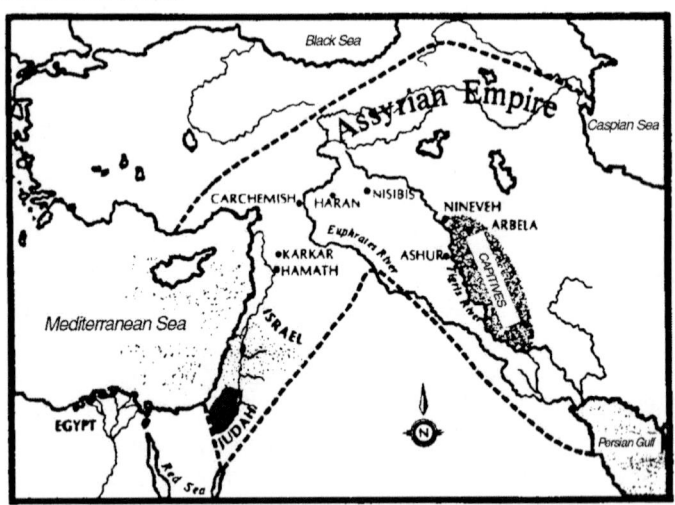

Application

3 Study the preceding map carefully. You can see how tremendous the Assyrian Empire was when compared to little Israel and Judah. The map shows that the captives were taken to a place
a) south of Nineveh and east of the Tigris river.
b) between the Tigris and Euphrates rivers.
c) located on the west side of the Persian Gulf.

Judgment and Captivity

But though we know where the ten tribes were taken, no account tells us what became of them after that. They simply disappear from history, never returning to their native land. Remember, however, that righteous members of every tribe had fled to Judah when the northern kingdom's first ruler, Jeroboam, had introduced idolatry. And probably some individuals who had been part of the northern kingdom returned to Jerusalem in the restoration we will study in Lesson 10.

Application

4 List in order the events of the fall of the northern kingdom. Write 1 before the one that happened first, 2 before the one that happened next, and so forth.

.... **a** Shalmaneser III extended Assyria's kingdom.

.... **b** The ten tribes were taken to Assyria.

.... **c** Assyria became the most powerful nation of the area.

.... **d** Sargon II captured Samaria.

.... **e** A three-year siege was made against Samaria.

The Fall of the Southern Kingdom

The fall of their northern brothers was a tremendous warning and message from God to Judah. And for a variety of reasons, including God's intervention, Judah did not fall to Assyria at this time.

Application

5 Read 2 Kings 19:32–36 and Isaiah 36–37. How did God intervene to keep Judah from falling to the Assyrians?

....

In time, however, Assyria itself fell to Babylon, who took over all its area. The prophet Nahum had predicted this. Nineveh, the capital city of Assyria and the place where Jonah had preached, was destroyed by Babylon in 612 B.C. Then Egypt challenged Babylon for possession of the western area of the fallen Assyrian empire. This included the territory in which little Judah, the southern kingdom, then stood alone. But Babylon remained supreme. God raised up strong prophetic voices such as Isaiah, Jeremiah, Nahum, Habakkuk, and Zephaniah during this period.

The southern kingdom failed to completely repent, although there were some bright spots of revival. Finally, the Lord used the Babylonians against Judah as He had used the Assyrians against Israel. The prophecies of Isaiah and Jeremiah tell the reasons for God's judgment. Judah's struggle against Babylon lasted about 20 years. Then the southern kingdom was taken captive to Babylon in three sections:

1. *605 B.C.* Nebuchadnezzar captured king Jehoiakim, the princes (Daniel and his companions) and the mighty men (2 Chronicles 36:5–6; Daniel 1:1–6). This is sometimes called the first captivity.

2. *598 B.C.* Nebuchadnezzar took king Jehoiachin and 10,000 leading citizens to Babylon (2 Kings 24:14–16). The prophet Ezekiel and the great-grandfather of Mordecai, Esther's cousin, were also taken captive at this time.

3. *586 B.C.* Jerusalem and the temple were burned and destroyed. Most of the remaining people were taken to Babylon (2 Kings 25:7–9).

Application

6 Study the following map. This time, the captives were taken to a place
a) on the northern border of the Babylonian empire.
b) in the area of the Tigris-Euphrates river valley.
c) near the southern shore of the Caspian sea.

Judgment and Captivity

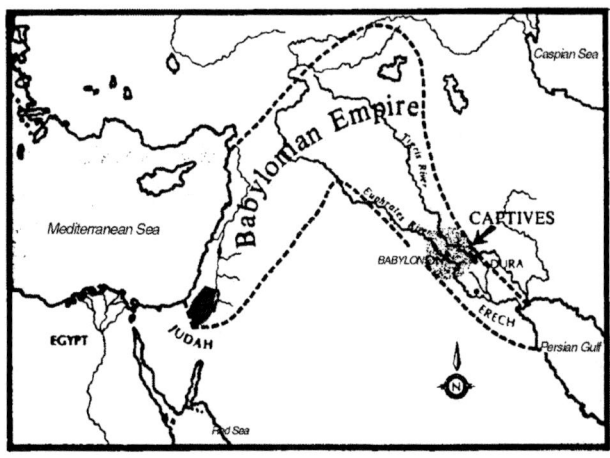

The southern kingdom had a better fate than the northern. It was punished by trouble and exile, yet later a remnant did return and Jerusalem was rebuilt. (We will study this restoration in Lesson 10.) But the nation would never again have the glory and power it did during the days of David and Solomon; never again, that is, until Jesus Christ returns to establish His glorious, lasting kingdom. Of His government there will be no end (Revelation 11:15)!

Application

7 List in order the events of the fall of the southern kingdom. Write 1 before the one that happened first, 2 before the one that happened next, and so forth.

... **a** Daniel and his companions were taken to Babylon.

... **b** Jerusalem and the temple were burned and destroyed.

... **c** The southern kingdom was warned by the fall of the northern kingdom to Assyria.

... **d** King Jehoiachin and Ezekiel were taken captive to Babylon.

... **e** Nineveh fell to the Babylonians.

THE EXPERIENCE OF CAPTIVITY

Objective 2. *Give details on the captivity, the leaders that God raised up during it, and the lessons God's people learned from it.*

The destruction of Jerusalem and the temple must have seemed like the end of the world to devout Jews. It was the ruin of all their hopes and the apparent triumph of the ungodly. Perhaps they felt that God had forgotten His people. But He had not!

Descriptions of Captivity

Four main writings in the Old Testament are closely associated with the years of the Babylonian captivity: Esther, Jeremiah, Ezekiel, and Daniel. These books help us understand what happened during those years.

The Jewish captives were settled in colonies at various points of the Babylonian empire. The previous map shows where the general area of settlement was. One group, with whom Ezekiel lived, was by the Chebar river (Ezekiel 1:1). Other groups formed special sections in larger towns, even in Babylon itself! The Jewish captives married, cultivated the ground, and became traders and business people. They eventually even owned houses and seemed to enjoy as much liberty as the other people of the country.

Application

8 Read Jeremiah 29:4–7. Notice what God told the captives to do. Why do you think God wanted them to do these things?

....

In fact, from the stories of Daniel and Esther we discover that some Jewish captives rose to positions of great authority within both the Babylonian and Medo-Persian empires. Such good treatment did not make most of them happy, though. They were captives in a foreign land. Their nation, their home, and their temple were desolate. Psalm 137 is a moving description of their feelings at this time.

Application

9 Read Psalm 137 once silently; then read it aloud. This is a song of lament. What special place did the captives vow to never forget?

....

Leaders During Captivity

God did not leave His scattered people without a message during their captivity. He raised up strong leaders among them. Daniel and Ezekiel are two examples of these. Both were from Judah, and both were taken captive to Babylon. Daniel was taken in the first group, and Ezekiel in the second.

Daniel was a princely young man who rose quickly into favor with Nebuchadnezzar, the king of Babylon. The book which records Daniel's experiences is rich in both history and prophecy. God allowed Daniel to predict the future kingdoms of the earth and to see the coming of the Messiah both to suffer and ultimately to reign as King of kings and Lord of lords.

Application

10 Read Daniel, chapters 1–3, and 9. Then answer the following questions in your notebook.
a) What plan did Daniel propose to Ashpenaz so that he could be faithful to God's will concerning food and drink?
b) How did Daniel show his faith in God when Nebuchadnezzar tested the wise men concerning his dream?
c) What was the result of the experience Shadrach, Meshach, and Abednego had in the blazing furnace?

Ezekiel was a young priest. God raised him up to witness to the captives that there was more judgment to come. When he began his ministry, Jerusalem and the temple had not yet been completely destroyed. For four and one-half years he preached the message of coming judgment. Then he retired to rest for two years until Jerusalem was destroyed. This fulfillment of his prophecy showed him to be a man of God. Later, God allowed Ezekiel to have the privilege of receiving marvelous visions of the ultimate reign of the Messiah and of the glorious future for all the true people of God. Read Ezekiel chapters 3–5, 7, 11, 33, 37, and 47 before continuing. Make a check mark here when you have completed your reading:

....

Application

11 Answer the following questions in your notebook.
a) According to chapters 3–5, how did God have Ezekiel give the message of the destruction of Jerusalem to the captives?
b) According to chapter 37, what vision did God give Ezekiel to show him that He would bring His people back to their land?
c) Compare Ezekiel 47 to Revelation 22:1–3. What do you think is represented by the river that Ezekiel saw?

Jeremiah continued to write and prophesy during this period. He was a greatly honored man, now that his prophecies had come true. For some reason he was allowed to remain in Judah and later went with the Israelites who fled into Egypt. His message also contained encouragement and hope for restoration; as we have seen, he predicted the return of the exiles to Jerusalem. Review and read Jeremiah chapters 29–31, 42, 50–52 before continuing. Make a check mark here when you have completed your reading:

....

Esther was another person of the captivity period. The Babylonian empire was defeated by the Persians, and Esther lived during the time following this defeat. The Persian king Xerxes (also called Ahasuerus) was the ruler. She became his queen and because of her obedience to God and her courage, the Jews of her day were spared from destruction. Her story, like that of Ruth, is one showing God's providence.

Application

12 Read Esther chapters 1–10. Especially notice 4:12–14. Can you make a comparison between your situation and Esther's? In your notebook, write down any lessons you can learn from her experience.

13 ....
Match each statement (left side) to the name of the prophet or person it describes (right side).

... **a** Saw a vision of a statue which represented the future of the world's kingdoms

... **b** Helped save the Jews from being killed because of Haman's plan

... **c** Was a priest and prophet who preached the downfall of Jerusalem for four and one-half years

... **d** Was a high official in the court of king Nebuchadnezzar of Babylon

... **e** Asked the Persian king, Xerxes, to stop the plan to kill the Jews

... **f** Sent a letter to the exiles in Babylon

1) Daniel
2) Ezekiel
3) Jeremiah
4) Esther

Results of Captivity

Although the years of captivity were bitter and difficult, there were many good results that came from them. Among these results were the following five benefits.

Purification from idolatry. God had judged His people for their idolatry by allowing them to be taken into captivity. But during their exile, they became aware of His presence in a new way. Unlike the gods of Assyria, Babylonia, and Egypt, who ceased to exist when their nations fell, the God of Israel was as powerful as ever. God's people saw His prophecies come to pass and experienced His distinct blessing on their lives. Their judgment actually became a spiritual victory; they never again showed a tendency to worship idols.

A new form of worship. Because there was no temple or tabernacle in the land of their captivity, the Israelites began holding meetings to read and discuss the Scriptures they possessed. This was the birth of the synagogue, a meeting place for worship. In the synagogue, people experienced a kind of teaching which led to closer relationships among them. This new form of worship was maintained even later when the temple had been restored. It greatly strengthened the faith of God's people.

A greater idea of God. Because they had been exiled from Palestine, the Israelites no longer thought of their land and temple as the only dwelling place of God. Their idea of God was enlarged. They began to receive God's message of a coming messiah! The idea that God would rule over the whole earth became more real to them.

A miraculous preservation. God supernaturally preserved a remnant of His people for the return to Jerusalem. This preservation was a miracle. They were not absorbed among the people of their land of captivity, as conquered nations had been before.

An effort to preserve the Scriptures. Another significant result of the captivity was that it produced an effort to gather together and preserve the sacred writings of the men whom God had inspired. This result has certainly brought great benefits to us today!

Application

14 Read 2 Kings 19:31. In this prophecy God promised that

a) there would be a group of survivors from Jerusalem.
b) all the captives of Judah would return to Zion.
c) more people would return to Jerusalem than had left it.

15 Which statement gives the most complete description of the benefits God's people gained from their years of bondage and captivity?

a) After their years of captivity, the Israelites did not worship idols as they had done before. They realized that though their nation had fallen, the God of Israel was still their God and had not been defeated.
b) Though they had been taken captive into a foreign nation they were miraculously preserved by God from losing their identity as a distinct people. This preservation made it possible for them to one day return to Jerusalem.
c) They turned away from idolatry and their ideas about God were enlarged. They began new ways of worship and were preserved by God so they could return to their land. They began collecting and preserving the Scriptures.

As the years went by, the people of God became aware of the great purposes God had in allowing them to undergo judgment and endure captivity. They no longer had doubts about God's majesty and supremacy. They had learned a wonderful but costly lesson.

self-test

1 Of the three great world powers during the years of God's judgment on Israel, the one located south and west of Palestine was
a) Assyria.
b) Babylon.
c) Egypt.

2 Circle the letter in front of each TRUE statement.
a) Samaria was captured after being besieged by Babylon for 3 years.
b) Jerusalem fell to the Assyrians in 586 B.C.
c) The Assyrian empire was taken over by the Babylonian empire.
d) The Babylonian empire was not as large as the Assyrian.

3 Arrange the following events in their correct order. Write 1 before the one which occurred first, 2 before the one which occurred next, and so forth.

.... **a** Babylon was defeated by the Persians.

.... **b** Jerusalem fell to king Nebuchadnezzar.

.... **c** God intervened to keep Jerusalem from falling to the Assyrians.

.... **d** Sargon II conquered Samaria.

.... **e** The prophet Ezekiel was taken captive.

.... **f** Esther persuaded king Xerxes to let the Jews defend themselves.

4 Suppose you were teaching a group of people that it is important for us to obey God's will in matters concerning the care of our bodies. Which of the following would provide the best example?
a) Ezekiel's vision of the dry bones
b) Daniel's explanation of king Nebuchadnezzar's dream
c) Daniel's success with Ashpenaz
d) Esther's influence on king Xerxes

5 Read each statement concerning the years of judgment and captivity (left side). Then decide whether it represents a description of a *reason* for judgment, a *means* God used in bringing judgment, or a *benefit* that was a result of judgment (right side).

... **a** The Babylonians laid siege to Jerusalem and destroyed it.

... **b** The southern kingdom did not fully repent even after the northern kingdom fell.

... **c** Idolatry was widespread among both the kings and the people.

... **d** Synagogues were started where Jews discussed the Scriptures.

... **e** God's people gained a new understanding of His power and supremacy.

1) Reason
2) Means
3) Benefit

answers to study questions

8 Because He wanted them to be strong and able to return to their land when the years of captivity were over (or a similar answer)

1 a) False
 b) True
 c) False

9 Jerusalem

2 Judgment came because they worshipped other gods, followed the customs of the Canaanites, and did things God disliked (or a similar answer).

10 a) That he be allowed to follow God's command for ten days so as to prove to Ashpenaz that it brought health.
 b) He asked for time to find out about the dream and prayed to God to reveal its mystery to him.
 c) The king praised the God of Israel and forbade people to speak disrespectfully of Him.

(Your answers should be similar.)

3 a) south of Nineveh and east of the Tigris river.

11 a) He had him act out the siege using various objects and motions.
 b) He had a vision of a valley of dry bones which were revived.
 c) It could represent the presence of God in giving life and healing.

(These are suggested answers. Yours may be similar or slightly different,)

4 a 1
 b 5
 c 2
 d 4
 e 3

Judgment and Captivity **233**

12 Your answer. Sometimes God allows us to have a position of favor or authority so we can be a special influence for good. This was true of Esther's life.

5 An angel of the Lord killed the Assyrian soldiers.

13 a 1) Daniel
  b 4) Esther
  c 2) Ezekiel
  d 1) Daniel
  e 4) Esther
  f 3) Jeremiah

6 b) in the area of the Tigris-Euphrates river valley.

14 a) there would be a group of survivors from Jerusalem.

7 a 3
  b 5
  c 1
  d 4
  e 2

15 c) They turned away from idolatry . . . . (The other two answers each mention only one of the benefits.)

LESSON 10 Return and Restoration

The glorious temple was in ruins, the beauty of Jerusalem had become a blackened circle of earth, and God's people were captives in a foreign land. But the story does not end there!

God judges what He plans to restore. And though the judgment of the Israelites was an inescapable result of their sin, it was only a preliminary step towards their future restoration. Its purpose was to teach and develop them. They had learned and developed through it.

But the seventy years of captivity came to an end, and God's purpose for Israel continued to be fulfilled; He restored His people to their homeland as He had promised. His covenant was eternal. It was an exciting time of new beginnings. Their experience gives us lessons of hope and encouragement today concerning the value of discipline and the possibility of restoration.

Like the Israelites we, too, can be called upon to restore areas of our own lives and ministries for the Lord. Though failure brings discipline, repentance speeds the process of restoration. Let us study these events with this principle in mind, aware of our weaknesses but conscious of His strength.

lesson outline

The Purpose of Restoration
The Progress of Rebuilding
The Messages to Restorers
The Last Warning to God's People

lesson objectives

When you finish this lesson you should be able to:

- Explain why it was necessary for the Jews to return to Jerusalem.

- Describe the three expeditions the Jews made to Jerusalem to rebuild the temple and the city.

- Distinguish between the messages of Haggai and Zechariah.

- Summarize the message of the book of Malachi.

learning activities

1. Read from the books of Ezra, Nehemiah, Haggai, Zechariah, and Malachi as the lesson directs you to.

2. Study all parts of the lesson development, answering the study questions and checking your answers. Then take the self-test and check your answers to that also.

3. Complete the lesson and review Unit 3.

4. When you have reviewed Unit 3 (Lessons 9 & 10), complete Unit Student Report 3 and return Answer Sheet to your national GU office if you live outside the United States or to your local church's CED learning center coordinator if you live in the United States.

    (If you are currently incarcerated in a jail or prison in the United States, please mark your answers on the scantron answer sheet provided and send to the following address: CED, Global University, 1211 S. Glenstone Ave., Springfield, MO 65804.)

key words

abuses	expedition	restoration
decline	preliminary	scribe
decree	preservation	survive

lesson development

THE PURPOSE OF RESTORATION

Objective 1. *Explain why it was necessary for the Jews to return to Jerusalem.*

God had made an everlasting covenant with Abraham about his family and descendants. He had repeated the promise to David, making it even stronger. God would not allow the people to whom He had made these promises to be lost in the fall and defeat of earthly kingdoms.

Indeed, the time during which the world was controlled by empires of the East came to an end. Persia was the last great eastern empire. Its power was lost to the Macedonian empire, the first great kingdom of the West. Had the Jewish nation continued in captivity in the East it would not have survived the decline of the eastern powers. It would never have influenced the world. God brought His people to their land in just the right time.

He placed them at the center of world events—right between the old and the new. Assyria, Babylon, and Persia, all the old great powers, had ceased to exist. New empires of the West were beginning to rise. The preservation of God's people amid the war-storms which totally destroyed the great eastern empires is one of His greatest miracles. It shows us that the most powerful nations decay, but God and His cause and those He saves will never be destroyed. As the prophets foretold, the knowledge of God's spiritual kingdom was destined to cover the earth. Today we can be a living fulfillment of that prophecy.

Application

1 Read Jeremiah 25:11–12; 29:10 and Daniel 9:1–19. Then answer the following questions in your notebook.
a) What did Daniel read?
b) What did Daniel confess?
c) What did Daniel request?

2 In your notebook, write two or three sentences which explain why it was necessary for the Jews to return to Jerusalem.

The Progress of Rebuilding

In 538 B.C., Babylon, the mighty empire and strong city, fell to Cyrus of Persia. Cyrus had already subdued several eastern kingdoms, and now he had conquered Babylon. According to ancient records, he reversed the policies of the Assyrians and Babylonians in general, freeing all captive peoples to return to their native lands.

It was Cyrus whom God used to begin the process of return and restoration. He sent out an important decree concerning the rebuilding of the temple. It must have amazed the Jews to hear a non-Jew say that the Lord had made him ruler of the whole earth! It was this decree that marked the beginning of the time of restoration and rebuilding.

Application

3 Read Cyrus' decree in Ezra 1:1-4 and answer the following questions in your notebook.
a) What responsibility did Cyrus say that God had given him?
b) In what way did he tell the people of Persia to help the Jews?

The Three Expeditions

Objective 2. *Describe the three expeditions the Jews made to Jerusalem to rebuild the temple and the city.*

The process of return and rebuilding covered a time span of about 100 years total. Beginning with Cyrus, other Persian kings were also involved. During these years there were three major expeditions of Jews from Persia to Israel. The books of Ezra and Nehemiah describe the events that occurred.

Return and Restoration

Notice the major facts related to each expedition which are summarized in the following chart. After the chart you will find a general description of each of these expeditions.

Biblical Record	First Expedition (538–536 B.C.) Ezra 1–6		Second Expedition (458–457 B.C.) Ezra 7–10	Third Expedition (445–444 B.C.) Nehemiah 1–13
Persian King	Cyrus	*Pause of 59 years. Persian kings during this time: Kambyses, Darius 1, and Xerxes 1.*	Artaxerxes	Artaxerxes
Jewish Leader	Zerubbabel and Jeshua		Ezra	Nehemiah
Total Number	49,697 returned		1,758 returned	An army escort
Events	Temple begun; sacrifices and feasts started. Temple finished in 516 B.C.		Revival of the law and worship	Wall rebuilt and dedicated; law read
Problems	Opposition of the Samaritans		Intermarriage with non-Jews	Opposition of Sanballat, Tobiah, and Geshem
Prophets	Haggai and Zechariah			
Time Span	Stage 1 20 years 536–516 B.C.		Stages 2 and 3 25 years 457–432 B.C.	

Application

4 Circle the letter of each TRUE statement.
a) The wall was rebuilt during the third expedition.
b) Artaxerxes was the Persian king when the first expedition took place.
c) More people returned in the second expedition than the first.
d) Tobiah opposed the building of the wall.

The First Expedition; Read Ezra 1–6

The number who are counted as returning with Zerubbabel might well represent only heads of families. Actually there might have been many more people. Nevertheless, the total number was still a small percentage of the Jews remaining in captivity. Many of them were prosperous and settled. They were not anxious to go back to Palestine to form a struggling little nation.

Application

5 Read Ezra 1:5. What did all the people who returned to Jerusalem have in common?

....

The journey was difficult and took at least four months. (Later on when Ezra came it took him four months according to Ezra 7:9). They arrived and began rebuilding the temple. The altar was set up and the foundation of the temple was laid (Ezra 3). Stones were available, but the wooden timbers had to be brought from Lebanon.

There was much opposition from enemies, and for 16 years the rebuilding of the temple stopped (Ezra 4). During this time God used the prophets Haggai and Zechariah to inspire the people to begin working again. The people responded, and the temple was completed and dedicated in about 516 B.C. (Ezra 5–6).

The Second Expedition; Read Ezra 7–10

Ezra, a scribe and priest, led the second expedition from Babylon to Jerusalem about sixty years after the temple had been completed (Ezra 7). He came with letters from king Artaxerxes which told the neighboring officials to offer protection and material help to God's people.

Ezra, who was a descendant of the house of Aaron, had a mission which was primarily spiritual. He brought along with him a number of priests. When he arrived he discovered heartbreaking abuses in the worship and practice of the people who had settled in Jerusalem. He stopped these abuses and made many reforms. A short outline of the events of this expedition is as follows:

Permission Granted to Ezra	Ezra 7–8:31
Arrival and Sacrifices	Ezra 8:32–36
Reform, Repentance, and Revival	Ezra 9–10

Application

6 Read Ezra 9–10 and answer the following questions in your notebook.
a) In what major way had the people disobeyed God?
b) Why was this disobedience so serious?

The Third Expedition; Read Nehemiah 1–13

Nehemiah is one of the greatest characters of the Bible. As cupbearer or wine steward to King Artaxerxes he held a high position in the Persian court. Because of his position he had great political power. He was told that conditions in Jerusalem were not good, and he asked permission to go to rebuild the city. Artaxerxes granted his request, and he traveled to Jerusalem accompanied by a group of soldiers the king had sent. His position, along with his godly character, made it possible for him to strengthen the Jews.

In only 52 days the walls of Jerusalem were rebuilt in spite of the opposition from the enemies of the Jews. After the walls were rebuilt Nehemiah took steps to bring stability and increase the number of people who lived in Jerusalem (Nehemiah 7:4–5; 11:1–2). He caused the wealthy Jews to stop oppressing the poor (Nehemiah 5:10) and introduced other reforms. But his greatest work was to re-establish the national life of the Jews upon the foundation of the written law (Nehemiah 10:28–39). The following is a brief outline of the book of Nehemiah:

Nehemiah's Arrival and Reforms	Nehemiah 1–7
Revival of Worship and Law	Nehemiah 8–10 Under Ezra
Lists of the Various Families	Nehemiah 11:1–12:26
Dedication of the Wall	Nehemiah 12:27–13:31

Application

7 Read Nehemiah 4 and 6. In your notebook, write how Nehemiah responded to each way that his enemies tried to stop him.
a) Ridicule (4:1–6)
b) Plans to attack him (4:7–23)
c) The first four messages of Sanballat and Geshem (6:1–4)
d) The fifth message of Sanballat (6:5–9)
e) The advice of Shemaiah (6:10–14)

8 According to Nehemiah 6:15–7:1, what was the final result of Nehemiah's efforts?

. . . .

9 Match each sentence (left side) to the expedition it most closely described (right side).

... **a** The Jews finished the temple.

... **b** Nehemiah received threatening letters from those who opposed the rebuilding.

... **c** The wall was completed and dedicated.

... **d** Ezra told the people that foreign wives must be put away.

... **e** Cyrus commanded God's people to rebuild the temple.

1) The first expedition
2) The second expedition
3) The third expedition

Return and Restoration

THE MESSAGES TO RESTORERS

Objective 3. *Distinguish between the messages of Haggai and Zechariah.*

As we have seen, the task of rebuilding and spiritual rebirth had much opposition. There were those on the outside who did not want to see God's work restored, and there were those on the inside who became easily discouraged. But during this time of rebuilding God had a word for His people. Both Haggai and Zechariah prophesied during the years the temple was being rebuilt. Their messages were meaningful to the people at the time they were given and also have marvelous insights into the future.

Haggai

Work on the rebuilding of the temple had ceased for almost ten years when Haggai gave his first message. He rebuked the people for their lack of concern for God's house. Read Haggai 1–2 before continuing. Make a check mark here when you have completed your reading:

....

Application

10 Review Haggai 1:2–11 and answer the following questions.
a) What were the people doing instead of finishing the temple?

....
b) What was the result of their actions?

....

The dramatic promises God gave the prophet Haggai stirred the people to begin rebuilding. But soon they became discouraged again, and God had another message for them.

Application

11 Read Haggai 2:1–9. According to this prophecy, God said that the new temple would be
a) equal in splendor to the old.
b) greater in splendor than the old.
c) filled with treasures from the nations.

Zechariah

The book of Zechariah, though only fourteen chapters long, contains some of the most important prophecies of the Old Testament The rebuilding which had begun after the people had responded to Haggai's message had been stopped. It was during this time that Zechariah received a series of eight visions concerning the reasons why the rebuilding had stopped (Zechariah 1–8). He was also given glorious promises of the future (Zechariah 9–14). Read Zechariah 1–14 before continuing. Make a check mark here when you have completed your reading:

. . . .

The message of the eight visions was received by Zechariah two months after the cornerstone of the temple had been laid. Among the reasons why the rebuilding had stopped were the following:

1. A sense of hopelessness and futility. The Jews saw themselves as unimportant. They felt they were doing something which really did not matter. But God said that He himself would come to Jerusalem and would claim the city as His own (1:17).

2. The results of sin and disobedience. God showed Zechariah that He would overthrow the nations that He had allowed to bring judgment upon His people (1:20–21).

3. A realization of condemnation and guilt. God showed Zechariah the high priest Joshua dressed in dirty garments

being accused by Satan. But Joshua's garments were replaced by new ones, and God promised to remove the guilt of the land (3:5, 9).

4. A feeling of powerlessness. Zechariah was given a message of encouragement for Zerubbabel and all others: "'Not by might nor by power, but by my Spirit'" (Zechariah 4:6).

Besides these visions there were others, such as the man with the measuring line (2:1–5). In this vision, the time when Jerusalem would be fully inhabited was prophesied. Also important in this first part of the book of Zechariah is a prophecy of the righteous "Branch," of whom Joshua was a picture (6:12–13).

In the second part of the book (chapters 9–14) there are other messages about the Messiah and the future of God's people. Israel will be cleansed (13:1), and one day all nations will worship the Lord (14:9).

Application

12 Review Zechariah 6:9–13. What would be the work of the man called the "Branch"?

. . . .

13 Review the foregoing summaries of Haggai and Zechariah. Match each sentence or verse (left side) to its corresponding book (right side).

... **a** "My people, why should you be living in well-built houses while my Temple lies in ruins?"

... **b** "I have taken away your sin and will give you new clothes to wear."

... **c** The descendants of David will be purified by the Lord.

... **d** "I sent scorching winds and hail to ruin everything you tried to grow."

... **e** Through a series of eight visions a message of encouragement was given.

1) Haggai
2) Zechariah

Often we are called upon to restore in our lives things that have been lost. Sometimes we need to begin again to have times of worshipping God together as families. On other occasions we may be called upon to help re-establish the broken ministry of a brother or sister in the Lord. The lessons from this section of the Bible are a great help in those times.

Application

14 Has the Lord been speaking to you about a certain work of restoration or rebuilding that you need to do? If so, write in your notebook a description of what needs to be done.

THE LAST WARNING TO GOD'S PEOPLE

Objective 4. *Summarize the message of the book of Malachi.*

The book of Malachi is sometimes called the "little Old Testament" because it contains in short form several of the major themes of the Old Testament: God's choice of Israel,

Israel's sins and disobedience, the importance of obeying the law, and the coming of the day of the Lord. It is probable that Malachi wrote his message after many years had passed following the return of the Jews to Jerusalem. Their first enthusiasm had left them. They were again religiously cold and morally loose. Read Malachi 1–4 before continuing. Make a check mark here when you have completed your reading:

....

Application

15 Read Malachi 3:6–12. The reason why there was a curse on the nation was because they had
a) brought no tithes and offerings to God.
b) neglected to come to worship in the temple.
c) not brought the full amount of tithes and offering.

Malachi spoke as a reformer, yet he also encouraged the people of God with a vision of the future. He prophesied that "the prophet Elijah" would appear before the coming of the day of the Lord (Malachi 3:1, 4:5). Four centuries of silence passed. But when God's time came, *the prophet Elijah* appeared to introduce the Messiah, Jesus (Matthew 11:10, 14).

Application

16 According to Malachi 4:1–3, "the day" of the Lord refers to the time when God
a) destroys the wicked and heals the righteous.
b) sends the prophet Elijah once again.
c) gives warnings to those who are evil.

17 Which of the following are TRUE statements about the message of Malachi?
a) According to Malachi's message, God did not answer the prayers of the people because they brought Him no offerings.
b) Malachi's message contained a rebuke of the sins of the Priests and a prophecy that evil people would be destroyed.
c) In his message, Malachi said that God was displeased because the people showed no respect for His altar.
d) The message of Malachi was that Jerusalem was going to be destroyed because of the sins of the people

---

The Old Testament is rich in meaning for us today. I hope this course has helped you to understand its message of trust in the living God. He is still the same today as He was when He walked in the Garden with Adam and Eve, called Abraham to serve Him, brought His people out of Egypt with mighty wonders, talked with Moses face to face, inspired king David to write the Psalms, and spoke through the lives and words of His servants the prophet. As you continue to read and study the Old Testament and its record of the experiences of God's people remember this:
"These things happened to them as examples and were written down as warnings for us, on whom the fulfillment of the ages has come" (1 Corinthians 10:11).

self-test

1 God preserved His people and brought them back to their land because
a) Assyria no longer was the ruler of the world.
b) Cyrus gave them instructions to build the temple.
c) they had a message to give to the whole world.
d) the world was controlled by empires of the East.

2 Which of the following statements is the best summary of all three stages in the progress of rebuilding?
a) In spite of much opposition from outside and discouragement from inside both the temple and the wall of Jerusalem were rebuilt. This took place over about 100 years under the leadership of Zerubbabel, Jeshua, Ezra, and Nehemiah. Obedience to the law and worship in the temple were revived.
b) Along with an army escort, Nehemiah returned to Jerusalem with letters from king Artaxerxes. He organized the people, and they were able to rebuild the wall in spite of their enemies who ridiculed them and made plans to stop them. The wall was then dedicated and the law was read.
c) During the reign of Artaxerxes Ezra returned with 1,758 people to Jerusalem. He found that the Jews had married foreign wives. He had them put these wives away and corrected the wrong practices the people were following. There was a revival of worship under his direction.

3 In question 2 above, which statement describes the events of the second expedition?
a) Statement a
b) Statement b
c) Statement c

4 Suppose you wanted to encourage a group of people to continue working for the Lord even though they were experiencing opposition. Which of the following would be good to use as an example?

a) Ezra's plan for ending marriages with foreign women
b) Zechariah's vision of the man with the measuring line
c) Ezra's revival of the law and worship during the second expedition
d) Nehemiah's experience during the rebuilding of the wall

5 Match the name of the person (right side) to each phrase which describes him (left side).

... **a** Wrote the description of the first and second expeditions

... **b** Gave the first decree for the Jews to rebuild the temple

... **c** Appeared in one of Zechariah's visions as receiving new garments

... **d** Was the Persian king during the third expedition

... **e** Told the people they had cheated God of His full tithes and offerings

... **f** Supervised the rebuilding of the wall

... **g** Rebuked the people for neglecting the rebuilding of the temple

... **h** Was given a series of eight visions concerning the rebuilding

... **i** Prophesied the coming of "the prophet Elijah"

... **j** Led the first expedition to Jerusalem

... **k** Was a Persian king who reigned between Cyrus and Artaxerxes

1) Artaxerxes
2) Cyrus
3) Darius
4) Ezra
5) Haggai
6) Joshua
7) Malachi
8) Nehemiah
9) Zechariah
10) Zerubbabel

> Be sure to complete your unit student report for Unit 3 and return the answer sheet to your GU instructor.

answers to study questions

9 a) 1) The first expedition
   b) 3) The third expedition
   c) 3) The third expedition
   d) 2) The second expedition
   e) 1) The first expedition

1 a) He read the prophecy God had given to Jeremiah concerning the years of captivity.
   b) He confessed the sins of his people,
   c) He asked God to restore the temple and to forgive the sins of the people because of His mercy.
(Your answers should be similar.)

10 a) They were building their own houses.
   b) God had caused their harvest to be small and drought to come upon the land.

2 God wanted the message concerning His kingdom to reach the entire world. By returning to Jerusalem, the people who had His message were saved from the destruction which came upon the nations who had held them as captives. In this way God kept His covenant with His people and preserved His message for the world.
(Your answer should be similar.)

11 b) greater in splendor than the old.
   c) filled with treasures from the nations.

3 a) To build a temple for the Lord in Jerusalem.
   b) To give them supplies for their trip and offerings for the Lord.

12 He would build the Lord's temple.

4 a) True
   b) False
   c) False
   d) True

13 a 1) Haggai 1:4
  b 2) Zechariah 3:4
  c 2) Zechariah 13:1
  d 1) Haggai 2:17
  e 2) Zechariah 1:7–6:8

 5 God stirred their hearts to return.

14 Your answer. Remember what God said to Zerubbabel. You, too, can be successful in the work of rebuilding.

  6 a) They had married foreign wives.
  b) Because it was forbidden by God and would lead the people back into idolatry and sinful practices.
(Your answers should be similar.)

15 c) not brought the full amount of tithes and offerings.

  7 a) He prayed and continued working.
  b) He told the people to trust in God and gave them weapons.
  c) He refused to meet them.
  d) He told them they were lying and prayed to God.
  e) He recognized that Shemaiah's advice was wrong, and he showed his trust in God.
(Your answers should be similar.)

16 a) destroys the wicked and heals the righteous.

 8 The wall was completely finished and the Levites were assigned to their work (or a similar answer).

  17 a) False
  b) True
  c) True
  d) False

Glossary

The right-hand column lists the lesson in the study guide in which the word is first used.

			Lesson
abuses	—	improper uses or treatments	10
A.D.	—	"in the year of our Lord"; occurring after the birth of Christ	1
allegiance	—	loyalty to someone or something; obligation due to a ruler	8
allegorical	—	having a supposed hidden spiritual meaning not found in the literal sense	7
alliance	—	a bond or connection between nations, families, or individuals	6
altar	—	a block of stone or structure on which an offering is placed	2
anointed	—	designated by a ceremony in which oil is poured on the head	6
antithetic	—	opposed to; in contrast to	7
Aramaic	—	the language common in Palestine after about 500 B.C.	1
assassination	—	the treacherous murder of a ruler or other person	8
Assyria	—	a powerful nation east of Palestine and north of Babylon	9
Babylon	—	a powerful nation east of Palestine and south of Assyria	9
B. C.	—	"before Christ"; occurring before Christ was born on earth	8
ceremonial law	—	laws relating to the priesthood, tabernacle, feasts, and offerings	4

Glossary

chronological	— arranged in order according to time	1
circumcision	— the physical sign of the covenant made on the male organ	3
civil law	— laws relating to property, marriage, and other similar aspects of life	4
civilization	— the culture of a certain group of people at a particular time or place	2
consecration	— the act or ceremony of devoting something to God	4
conviction	— the state of being persuaded of an error; strong belief	6
covenant	— a formal, solemn, and binding agreement	2
cross-section	— a representation of something as if it had been cut in half	5
crucial	— decisive; important or essential as to resolving a crisis	2
culture	— the customs, arts, conveniences of a civilization	3
current affairs	— events which are occurring at the present time	8
cycle	— a sequence in which certain events reoccur or are repeated	5
debauchery	— extreme indulgence in sensuality	5
Decalogue	— the Ten Commandments given to Israel	4
decline	— to diminish; to gradually waste away	10
decree	— an order usually having the force of a law	10
dethroned	— removed from being king or ruler	6
dynasty	— a succession of rulers from the same family or line of descent	8

era	— a period of time typified by some prominent feature	8
exile	— forced removal from one's country	9
expedition	— a journey taken for a specific purpose	10
feast	— a special ceremony held to mark the memory of a certain event	4
fertile crescent	— the land in the area of the Tigris and Euphrates rivers	2
genealogy	— an account of the ancestors of a certain person, family, or group	8
geographical	— having to do with the physical land	2
Greek	— the language in which the New Testament was written	1
Hebrew	— the language in which most of the Old Testament was written	1
history	— a chronological record of significant events	1
idols	— objects used to represent false gods	3
inhabitant	— one who lives in a certain place	5
inheritance	— property or money passed down within a family	5
inspiration	— the quality or state of having been moved or guided by God	1
interpretation	— the explanation or meaning of something	7
intervention	— the act of coming between to modify or change in some way	9
intimate	— marked by warm friendship developed through long association	7
invaders	— those who enter for conquest or spoil	5
kingdom	— a politically organized community headed by a king	6
league	— an association of nations for a common purpose	5

Glossary

legalism	—	literal or excessive conformity to the law; dependence on law for salvation	4
literature	—	writings having excellence in form and expression	1
manna	—	food miraculously supplied to the Israelites in their wilderness journey	4
manuscript	—	a handwritten document	1
Masoretes	—	a group of Jewish scholars who were responsible for preserving the Old Testament	1
Messiah	—	the name given to Jesus as the one chosen by God to do a special work	4
migrate	—	to move from one country or place to another	3
moral law	—	laws having to do with basic principles of right and wrong	4
obligation	—	a duty or responsibility toward something or someone	6
offering	—	a sacrifice given as part of worship	4
origin	—	the point at which something begins	2
parallel	—	extending in the same direction keeping the same distance apart	5
parallelism	—	the quality or state of having similar elements in similar positions	7
patriarch	—	one of the fathers of the Hebrew people	3
peninsula	—	a piece of land surrounded on three sides by water	4
philosophy	—	a system of beliefs and attitudes	7
plague	—	a disastrous evil or affliction	3
plateau	—	land having a level surface but higher than the surrounding land	5
poem	—	a literary piece or writing in verse	7

poetry	—	writing in verse	1
political	—	of or relating to government	8
prediction	—	something declared before it happens	8
preliminary	—	something that is introductory or preparatory	10
preservation	—	the quality of having been kept from injury, destruction, or harm	10
priest	—	one who has been given the authority to perform religious ceremonies	4
prophecy	—	a message given from God to man	1
prosperity	—	the state of being successful; economic well-being	6
providence	—	divine guidance or care	3
redemption	—	the act or process of buying back	2
reign	—	to possess or exercise power as a king or ruler	6
remnant	—	a small surviving group	8
restoration	—	a bringing back to a former position or condition	10
revelation	—	something made known by God to man	1
rhyme	—	to sound alike; a poem having certain words of similar sound	7
scribe	—	a man who studied the Scriptures and who served as a copyist and teacher	10
Septuagint	—	the Greek translation of the Old Testament made around 200-300 B.C.	1
siege	—	the act of surrounding a city and compelling it to surrender	9
successor	—	one that follows another, usually in holding a throne or office	5
supremacy	—	the state or quality of being the highest in rank, power, or authority	9
survive	—	to remain alive or in existence	10

synagogne	—	a Jewish congregation or group meeting for worship	9
synonynmous	—	alike in meaning or significance	7
synthetic	—	relating to something which is the result of a combination of parts	7
theme	—	a subject or topic of speech or writing	1
theocracy	—	government by immediate divine guidance	6
transition	—	a passage from one state to another	6
translated	—	having been put into a different language	7
translation	—	something which has been put into a different language	1
tribute	—	a payment by one ruler to another to show submission	8
ultimate	—	basic, fundamental	1
vassal	—	a person under the protection of another; one in a subordinate position	9
veil	—	a length of cloth worn as a covering over the face; a concealing curtain	4
vellum	—	fine-grained animal skin prepared for use as a writing surface	1
verbal	—	having to do with words	1
wisdom	—	deep understanding; keen insight	7
writing prophet	—	a prophet after whom an Old Testament book is named (such as Isaiah)	8

Answers to Self-Tests

Lesson 1

1 **c)** book of Psalms in the Bible.

2 **a)** breathed by God.

3 **c)** it is trustworthy and true throughout.

4 **a)** False
   b) False
   c) True
   d) True

5 **c)** record of the emotions and feelings of God's people.

6 **b)** Book B, which tells about events that happened before those described in both Book A and Book C.

7 **a)** The Masoretes were careful scholars who made accurate copies of the Scriptures.
   c) The Dead Sea Scrolls from 70 A.D. agree with the Old Testament manuscripts from 900 A.D.

8 **b)** Romans 4:11, 16, and 24 says that we are the spiritual descendants of Abraham.
   d) The entire Bible, including the Old Testament, is the Word of God.

Lesson 2

1 **a)** that God created the world from nothing.

2 **b)** have dominion over creation.

3 **d)**

4 **c)** humans cannot cover sin by their own efforts.

5 **b)** Adam and Eve listened to Satan's suggestion....

6 **a)** was just and walked with God.

7 **c)** north of the Persian gulf.

Answers To Self-Tests

8 **a)** 6
   b) 3
   c) 5
   d) 1
   e) 9
   f) 7
   g) 2
   h) 8
   i) 4

9 **a)** True
   b) False
   c) True

Lesson 3

1 **a)** They had rejected God's truth and were rebellious.

2 **c)** leave his native land.

3 **c)** Ur, Haran, Shechem

4 **b)** obedience

5 **b)** Jacob.

6 **a)** True
   b) True
   c) False
   d) True
   e) False
   f) False

Lesson 4

1 **a** 2) Civil law
   b 1) Moral law
   c 3) Ceremonial law
   d 1) Moral law
   e 2) Civil law

2. a) False
   b) True
   c) False

3. a) 2) Compulsory offerings
   b) 2) Compulsory offerings
   c) 2) Compulsory offerings
   d) 1) Voluntary offerings
   e) 1) Voluntary offerings
   f) 1) Voluntary offerings
   g) 1) Voluntary offerings
   h) 2) Compulsory offerings

4. a) believe what He has said.

5. c) they did not believe God.

6. b) Priesthood
   d) Tabernacle
   e) Sacrifices and offerings
   h) Position of the tribes
   j) Feasts and seasons

7. a) False
   b) True
   c) True
   d) False
   e) False

8. a) 3) Camp of Israel
   b) 1) Priesthood
   c) 2) Tabernacle
   d) 4) Sacrifices and offerings
   e) 5) Feasts and seasons

Answers To Self-Tests **263**

9 **a)** 5
  b) 7
  c) 1
  d) 8
  e) 6
  f) 2
  g) 3
  h) 4

Lesson 5

1 **a)** False
  b) True
  c) True
  d) False
  e) False

2 **b)** God had given the Canaanites a chance to repent. . . .

3 **c)** forgot the Lord and served idols.

4 **a)** God had great patience with the Israelites. . . .
  d) The judges needed God's help and direction. . . .

5 **a)** was her near relative.

6 **b)** near kinsman who restores.

7 **c)** great-grandmother.

8 **d)** God expects parents to correct and discipline their children.

9 **a** 2) Samuel
  b 2) Samuel
  c 1) Joshua
  d 3) Both
  e 2) Samuel
  f 1) Joshua
  g 3) Both

Lesson 6

1 **b)** His instructions were that the king was to obey His law...

2 **a** 2) David
 b 1) Saul
 c 3) Solomon
 d 2) David
 e 3) Solomon
 f 3) Solomon
 g 2) David
 h 1) Saul

3 **b)** David

4 **a)** 2
 b) 4
 c) 7
 d) 1
 e) 3
 f) 5
 g) 9
 h) 10
 i) 8
 j) 6

5 **a** 4) Solomon
 b 2) Saul
 c 1) Samuel
 d 4) Solomon
 e 3) David

Lesson 7

1 **a)** a wicked man's ideas are worthless.

2 **a)** True
 b) True
 c) False
 d) False
 e) False

Answers To Self-Tests

3 **e)** Song of Songs.

4 **b)** teach him new things about himself and God.

5 **b)** Psalms

6 **c)** applies wisdom to human relationships.

7 **a** 4) Psalm 66:1–2
   b 1) Job 34:32
   c 3) Ecclesiastes 1:14
   d 5) Song of Songs 8:13
   e 1) Job 42:5
   f 2) Proverbs 23:9

Lesson 8

1 **c)** Solomon turned away from God to worship idols.

2 **a)** True
   b) False
   c) False
   d) True
   e) False

3 **a)** describe the reign of Solomon.
   d) record the ministry of Elijah and Elisha.

4 **a** 2) Southern
   b 1) Northern
   c 1) Northern

5 **c)** The people and most of the kings did not faithfully follow God.

6 **a)** False
   b) True
   c) False
   d) False
   e) True

Lesson 9

1. **c)** Egypt
2. **a)** False
   b) False
   c) True
   d) True
3. **a)** 5
   b) 4
   c) 2
   d) 1
   e) 3
   f) 6
4. **c)** Daniel's success with Ashpenaz.
5. **a** 2) Means
   b 1) Reason
   c 1) Reason
   d 3) Benefit
   e 3) Benefit

Lesson 10

1. **c)** they had a message to give to the whole world.
2. **a)** in spite of much opposition. . . .
3. **c)** Statement c
4. **d)** Nehemiah's experience during the rebuilding of the wall

Answers To Self-Tests

5
- **a** 4) Ezra
- **b** 2) Cyrus
- **c** 6) Joshua
- **d** 1) Artaxerxes
- **e** 7) Malachi
- **f** 8) Nehemiah
- **g** 5) Haggai
- **h** 9) Zechariah
- **i** 7) Malachi
- **j** 10) Zerubbabel
- **k** 3) Darius 1

Appendix

KINGS AND PROPHETS
OF THE DIVIDED KINGDOM
Northern Kingdom: Israel

Year; King's Name and Bible Reference	Length of Reign and How Gained	Spiritual Character	Prophets
931; JEROBOAM 1 1 Kings 12:25—14:20	Chosen 22 years	Bad	**Ahijah**
910; Nadab 1 Kings 15:25–31	Inherited 2 years	Bad	
909; BAASHA 1 Kings 15:32—16:17	Assassination 24 years	Bad	**Jehu**
886; Elah 1 Kings 16:8–14	Inherited 2 years	Bad	
885; ZIMRI 1 Kings 16:15–20	Assassination 7 days	Bad	
885; OMRI 1 Kings 16:23–28	Army's Choice 12 years	Very Bad	**Elijah**
874; Ahab 1 Kings 16:29—22:40	Inherited 22 years	The Worst	**Micaiah**
853; Ahaziah 1 Kings 22:51— 2 Kings 10:18	Inherited 2 years	Bad	**Elisha**
852; Joram 2 Kings 1:17; 3:1—8:15	Inherited 12 years	Bad	
841; JEHU 2 Kings 9:30—10:36	Assassination 28 years	Bad	
814; Jehoahaz 2 Kings 13:1–9	Inherited 17 years	Bad	

Appendix

798; Jehoash 2 Kings 13:10–25	Inherited 16 years	Bad	**JONAH**
793; Jeroboam 2 2 Kings 14:23–29	Inherited 41 years	Bad	**HOSEA AMOS**
753; Zechariah 2 Kings 15:8–12	Inherited 6 months	Bad	
752; SHALLUM 2 Kings 15:13–15	Assassination 1 month	Bad	
752; MENAHEM 2 Kings 15:16–22	Assassination 10 years	Bad	
742; Pekahiah 2 Kings 15:23–26	Inherited 2 years	Bad	**Oded**
740; Pekah 2 Kings 15:27–31	Overthrow 20 years	Bad	
732; HOSHEA 2 Kings 15:30; 17:1–41	Assassination 9 years	Bad	
722; FALL OF SAMARIA			**MICAH**

Southern Kingdom: Judah

Year; King's Name and Bible Reference	Length of Reign	Spiritual Character	Prophets
Year?; Rehoboam 1 Kings 12:1–24; 14:21–31 2 Chronicles 11:1—12:16	17 years	Bad	
913; Abijah: 1 Kings 15:1–8 2 Chronicles 13:1–22	8 years	Bad	**Shemaiah**

910; Asa; 1 Kings 15:9–24; 2 Chronicles 14:1—16:14	41 years	Good	**Iddo Azariah**
870; Jehoshaphat; 1 Kings 22:41–50; 2 Chr. 17:1—21:1	25 years	Good	**Hanani**
848; Jehoram: 2 Kings 8:16–24; 2 Chronicles 21:2–20	8 years	Bad	**Eliezer**
841; Ahaziah; 2 Kings 8:25–29; 9:27–29; 2 Chr. 22:1–9	1 year	Bad	**Jehoiada**
841; Athaliah; 2 Kings 11:1–21; 2 Chr. 22:10—23:21	6 years	Very Bad	
835; Joash; 2 Kings 12:1–21; 2 Chronicles 24:1–27	40 years	Fairly Good	**ZECHARIAH**
796; Amaziah: 2 Kings 14:1–22; 2 Chronicles 25:1–28	29 years	Fairly Good	**JOEL**
790; Uzziah; 2 Kings 15:1–7; 2 Chronicles 26:1–3	52 years	Fairly Good	**AMOS**
750; Jotham; 2 Kings 15:30, 32–38; 2 Chronicles 27:1–9	16 years	Fairly Good	**ISAIAH**
735; Ahaz; 2 Kings 16:1–20; 2 Chronicles 28:1–27	16 years	Bad	
715; Hezekiah; 2 Kings 18:1—20:21; 2 Chr. 29:1—32:33	29 years	Very Good	**MICAH**

Year?; Manasseh; 2 Kings 21:1–18; 2 Chr. 33:1–20	55 years	The Worst	
642; Amon; 2 Kings 21:19–26; 2 Chronicles 33:21–25	2 years	Very Bad	
640; Josiah; 2 Kings 22:1—23:30; 2 Chr. 34:1—35:27	31 years	Very Good	**JEREMIAH** **Huldah**
609; Jehoahaz; 2 Kings 23:31–33; 2 Chr. 36:1–4	3 months	Bad	**ZEPHANIAH**
609; Jehoiakim; 2 Kings 23:34—24:7; 2 Chr. 36:5–8	11 years	Bad	**NAHUM**
598; Jehoiachin; 2 Kings 24:6–16; 2 Chronicles 36:9–10	3 months	Bad	**HABAKKUK**
597; Zedekiah; 2 Kings 24:18—25:26, 2 Chr. 36:11–21	11 years	Bad	**OBADIAH**
586; FALL OF JERUSALEM			

The length of each king's reign is identified in scripture (Column 2). These do not in every case correspond to the chronological time line (Column 1). This is the result of overlapping reigns and co-regencies.

Tents, Temples, and Palaces

UNIT STUDENT REPORTS AND ANSWER SHEETS

DIRECTIONS

When you have completed your study of each unit, fill out the unit student report answer sheet for that unit. The following are directions how to indicate your answer to each question. There are two kinds of questions: TRUE-FALSE and MULTIPLE-CHOICE.

TRUE-FALSE QUESTION EXAMPLE

The following statement is either true or false. If the statement is

  TRUE, blacken space A.

  FALSE, blacken space B.

1 The Bible is God's message for us.

The above statement, *The Bible is God's message for us,* is TRUE, so you would blacken space A like this:

1 ■ B C D

MULTIPLE CHOICE QUESTION EXAMPLE

There is one best answer for the following question. Blacken the space for the answer you have chosen.

2 To be born again means to
   a) be young in age.
   b) accept Jesus as Savior.
   c) start a new year.
   d) find a different church.

The correct answer is b) *accept Jesus as Savior,* so you would blacken space B like this:

2 | A | ■ | C | D |

STUDENT REPORT FOR UNIT ONE

Answer all questions on Answer Sheet for Unit One. See the examples on the DIRECTIONS *page which show you how to mark your answers.*

PART 1—TRUE-FALSE QUESTIONS

The following statement is either true or false. If the statement is

    TRUE, blacken space A.
    FALSE, blacken space B.

1 I have carefully read all of the lessons in Unit One.

2 The three main divisions of the Old Testament books are history, prophecy, and poetry.

3 In Christian teaching, the Fall refers to the time when Satan was cast out of heaven.

4 Eight people were saved when God destroyed the world with the Flood.

5 Abraham's first test of faith concerned sacrificing his son Isaac.

6 The land of Egypt was located in the area between the Tigris and Euphrates river.

7 Israel received the Law during the time they were camped at Mt. Sinai.

8 The entrance to the court or enclosure of the tabernacle was on the east side.

PART 2—MULTIPLE-CHOICE QUESTIONS

There is one best answer for each of the following questions. Blacken the space on your answer sheet for the answer you have chosen.

9 The basic theme or subject of the Old Testament is the
a) history of the beginning of civilization.
b) thoughts of good men who sought after truth.
c) revelation of God to man through His acts and words.
d) story of the kings of Israel.

10 The Old Testament books of history
a) have little to do with those of prophecy.
b) help one understand those of prophecy.
c) are more important than those of prophecy.
d) are not as important as those of prophecy.

11 According to the Genesis account of Creation, man was created
a) at the same time the animals were.
b) after the likeness of angels.
c) in the image of God.
d) before the animals were.

12 Which one of these events in Genesis pointed to the fact that one day a Savior would have to die for humanity's sins?
a) God clothed Adam and Eve with the skins of animals.
b) The serpent (Satan) tempted Eve to disobey God.
c) Adam and Eve were sent from the Garden.
d) The serpent (Satan) was cursed by God.

13 After a description of where Noah's descendants settled, the account in Genesis emphasizes the family of
a) Shem.
b) Ham.
c) Japheth.
d) Canaan.

14 According to Romans 1, the corrupted condition of humankind described in Genesis 6 and 11 was a result of their
a) ignorance of the truth.
b) desire for greater prosperity.
c) need for fuller knowledge.
d) rejection of the truth.

15 The issue involved when God called Abram to leave Ur was that of
a) power.
b) delay.
c) riches.
d) separation.

16 The Israelites put the Passover lamb's blood on their doorposts. Another action which had the same result was when
a) Abram's name was changed to Abraham.
b) Noah built the boat (or ark).
c) Isaac married Rebecca.
d) Abram migrated from Ur to Haran.

17 Which statement comes from the moral law which God gave to Israel?
a) Celebrate three festivals a year to honor Me.
b) Offer your food offerings to the Lord for seven days.
c) Respect your father and your mother.
d) No priest shall shave any part of his head.

18 The furnishing in the Tent of the Lord's Presence which most clearly pictured Christ's death for our sins was the
a) altar of sacrifice.
b) golden lampstand.
c) table of bread.
d) bronze basin.

19 It was only on the Day of Atonement that the high priest sprinkled the blood of the sacrifice on the
a) golden altar of incense.
b) mercy seat.
c) altar of sacrifice.
d) winged creatures.

20 One of the consequences of Israel's unbelief at Paran was that
a) only the priests and Levites were permitted to enter Canaan.
b) they had to wander in the wilderness for 60 years.
c) no one over 20 at the time entered Canaan later, except Joshua and Caleb.
d) all of the spies died in a plague.

END OF REQUIREMENTS FOR UNIT ONE. Follow the remaining instructions on your answer sheet and return it to your GU Instructor or office in your area, then begin your study of Unit Two.

STUDENT REPORT FOR UNIT TWO

Answer all questions on Answer Sheet for Unit Two. See the examples on the DIRECTIONS page which show you how to mark your answers.

PART 1—TRUE-FALSE QUESTIONS

The following statements are either true or false. If the statement is

    TRUE, blacken space A.
    FALSE, blacken space B.

1 I have carefully read all of the lessons in Unit Two.

2 In the history of Israel, the era of the Judges followed the era of the Kingdom.

3 In the land of Palestine, the Jordan river valley lies between the Mediterranean Sea and the central mountains.

4 The peoples' request for a king displeased God.

5 After Saul's death, David was recognized as king by all the tribes of Israel.

6 David, Moses, and Solomon were among the writers of the book of Psalms.

7 Of the two kingdoms, the northern kingdom went into captivity first.

8 The southern kingdom was ruled by nine separate dynasties.

PART 2—MULTIPLE-CHOICE QUESTIONS

There is one best answer for each of the following questions. Blacken the space on your answer sheet for the answer you have chosen.

9 Israel was commanded to destroy the Canaanites because the Canaanites
a) were not descendants of the righteous family of Noah.
b) had continued in sin and would teach Israel to sin.
c) had never had any knowledge of the true God.
d) were more numerous and prosperous than the Israelites.

10 Which sentence correctly describes an aspect of Joshua's seven-year war of conquest?
a) Joshua began by conquering the city of Hebron in the south and then went north.
b) Joshua first took Jericho and the central area; he then conquered the southern area and finally the northern area.
c) Joshua began by taking the northern area, then proceeded to take the central area and finally the southern part.
d) After conquering Jericho, Joshua went north to take Dan and then south to take Jerusalem.

11 When the land was divided among the tribes,
a) more tribes were located east of the Jordan river than west.
b) no tribes were located east of the Jordan river.
c) the tribes of Judah and Simeon were located in the southwest.
d) all the tribes had the same amount of territory.

12 The era of the Judges can best be described as the time when Israel
a) repeated cycles of sin, punishment, repentance, and deliverance.
b) had no leaders to deliver them from the oppressing nations.
c) ceased to repent or call upon God to deliver them.
d) had two periods of about 40 years of rest from their oppressors.

13 Saul was rejected as king because he
a) refused to offer sacrifices.
b) lacked military skill.
c) repeatedly disobeyed the Lord.
d) was disliked by the people.

14 The most important reason David pleased the Lord was that he
a) won many victories for Israel.
b) had been anointed by Samuel.
c) wrote many beautiful Psalms.
d) kept an attitude of humility and repentance.

15 Solomon was led into idolatry mainly because of the
a) alliances he made with other nations.
b) spiritual rebellion of the people.
c) lack of leadership among the priests.
d) influence of his foreign wives.

16 The book of Job can best be described as
a) a group of wise sayings concerning the behavior of young men.
b) many beautiful poems and songs of praise to the Lord.
c) a record of several speeches about the meaning of suffering.
d) the story of how Job lost all because he was a sinner.

17 The Jews likened the book of Proverbs to the outer court of the temple because it
a) was written by Solomon, who built the temple.
b) explained what the temple ceremonies meant.
c) contained advice concerning human relationships.
d) gave a description of the behavior required of priests.

18 The books 1 and 2 Chronicles place special emphasis on the
a) kings of Israel, the northern kingdom.
b) ceremonies and officials of the temple.
c) reign of the kings who obeyed the Lord.
d) ministries of the prophets such as Elijah and Elisha.

19 The kingdom was divided primarily because
a) Solomon turned away from the Lord.
b) Israel's enemies became too strong to defeat.
c) there were no godly prophets to warn the people.
d) none of David's descendants were able to rule.

20 The prophets' message is most completely described as
a) a detailed list of all principles of right and wrong which should be followed by all godly people.
b) a summary of past events and predictions of the future.
c) an explanation of all that would take place during the life and ministry of the Messiah.
d) a message for his own generation, predictions of the future, and moral principles for all godly people.

END OF REQUIREMENTS FOR UNIT TWO. Follow the remaining instructions on your answer sheet and return it to your GU instructor or office in your area, then begin your study of Unit Three.

STUDENT REPORT FOR UNIT THREE

Answer all questions on Answer Sheet for Unit Three. See the examples on the DIRECTIONS page which show you how to mark your answers.

PART 1—TRUE-FALSE QUESTIONS

The following statements are either true or false. if the statement is

    TRUE, blacken space A.
    FALSE, blacken space B.

1 I have carefully read all of the lessons in Unit Three.

2 The northern kingdom was defeated in 722 B.C. by the Assyrians.

3 The book of Daniel is associated with the years of the Babylonian captivity.

4 Esther asked the Egyptian king not to allow the Jews to be killed.

5 The decree for the Jews to rebuild the temple came from Cyrus, the king of Persia.

6 It was during the third expedition that most of the Jews returned to Jerusalem.

7 The Jews had no opposition to their task of rebuilding the wall of Jerusalem.

8 The Jews were not able to completely finish the wall of Jerusalem.

PART 2—MULTIPLE-CHOICE QUESTIONS

There is one best answer for each of the following questions. Blacken the space on your answer sheet for the answer you have chosen.

9 In relation to foreign powers, the divided kingdoms were located

a) in a triangle with Assyria and Egypt on the west and Babylon on the east.

b) west of Egypt and closer to the Assyrian border than the Babylonian.

c) about halfway between the two great cities of Nineveh and Babylon.

d) in a triangle with Babylon and Assyria on the east and Egypt on the west.

10 Which sentence correctly describes the fall of the northern kingdom?

a) After a ten-year siege of Samaria, Sargon II took captives to Babylon.

b) Shalmaneser III captured the northern kingdom after a five-year siege of Samaria.

c) The northern kingdom resisted until 586 B.C. and then fell.

d) Sargon II captured Samaria after a five-year siege and took captives to Assyria.

11 Which sentence correctly describes the fall of the southern kingdom?

a) The southern kingdom fell to the Assyrians in 586 B.C.

b) Jerusalem was burned and destroyed by Nebuchadnezzar in 605 B.C.

c) After 20 years of resistance to Babylon, Jerusalem fell in 586 B.C.

d) Sargon II defeated the southern kingdom and took captives in 586 B.C.

12 The writings of God's people during their captivity show us that
a) God did not continue to give them prophecies about the Messiah.
b) some Jews had positions of great power and influence.
c) they had no real hope of ever returning to Jerusalem.
d) it was impossible for any of them to continue worshipping God.

13 Which books are most closely associated with the Babylonian captivity?
a) Esther, Jeremiah, Ezekiel, and Daniel
b) Ruth, Esther, Ezekiel, and Jeremiah
c) Isaiah, Daniel, Hosea, and Joel
d) Esther, Job, Daniel, and Ezekiel

14 According to Lesson 9, one of the five benefits gained by the Jews from their years of captivity was that they
a) learned about the culture of other civilizations.
b) began a new form of worship that birthed the synagogue.
c) enjoyed success and favor with all the foreign rulers.
d) settled down in the land of captivity and became prosperous.

15 The reason why God brought His people back to their land at the time He did was to
a) preserve them from the decline of the eastern empires.
b) give them rest from the increasing might of the Babylonians.
c) save them from the rising powers of the Persian empire.
d) help them survive the decline of the Macedonian empire.

16 In the first expedition of rebuilding,
a) Zerubbabel and Jeshua were the leaders, and the temple was rebuilt.
b) Cyrus told the Jews to rebuild and sent Nehemiah to lead them.
c) about 2,000 Jews returned and were successful in rebuilding the wall.
d) the wall was dedicated and Ezra brought about a revival of worship.

17 Haggai's message to those who were in Jerusalem contained a
a) vision concerning a man with a measuring line.
b) rebuke regarding their lack of concern for the temple.
c) prophecy about a man called the "Branch."
d) description of how the wall was rebuilt by Ezra.

18 A prophecy concerning the appearance of "the prophet Elijah" before the coming day of the Lord was given in
a) Nehemiah.
b) Haggai.
c) Zechariah.
d) Malachi.

19 After Exodus, the six eras of Israel's history in order are:
a) Conquest, Judges, Kingdom, Two Kingdoms, Judah Alone, Captivity.
b) Conquest, Judges, Two Kingdoms, Kingdom, Judah Alone, Captivity.
c) Conquest, Judges, Judah Alone, Kingdom, Two Kingdoms, Captivity.
d) Conquest, Judges, Kingdom, Judah Alone, Two Kingdoms, Captivity.

20 In studying the Old Testament, the most important thing to realize is that it
a) describes different events that happened before Christ came.
b) tells us about the customs of people that lived in Palestine.
c) reveals to us God's nature through His dealings with His people.
d) contains descriptions of Assyria, Babylon, and Egypt.

END OF REQUIREMENTS FOR UNIT THREE. Follow the remaining instructions in your answer sheet and return it to your GU instructor or office in your area. This completes your study of this course. Ask your GU instructor to recommend another course of study for you.

CS2221   Tents, Temples, and Palaces
UNIT ONE ANSWER SHEET

Congratulations on finishing your study of the lessons in Unit 1! Please fill in all the blanks below.

Your Name ....

Your GU Student Number ....
(Leave blank if you do not know what it is.)

Your Mailing Address ....

....

City ....

Province/State ....   Postal/Zip ....

Country ....

Occupation ....   Age ....
Sex................................

Are you married? .... How many members are in your family? ....

How many years have you studied in school? ....

Are you a member of a church? ....

If so, what is the name of the church? ....

What responsibility do you have in your church? ....

....

How are you studying this course: Alone? ....

In a group? ....

What other GU courses have you studied? ....

....

....

Answer Sheet for Unit One

Blacken the correct space for each numbered item. For all questions, be sure the number beside the spaces on the answer sheet is the same as the number of the question.

1	[A] [B] [C] [D]	8	[A] [B] [C] [D]	15	[A] [B] [C] [D]
2	[A] [B] [C] [D]	9	[A] [B] [C] [D]	16	[A] [B] [C] [D]
3	[A] [B] [C] [D]	10	[A] [B] [C] [D]	17	[A] [B] [C] [D]
4	[A] [B] [C] [D]	11	[A] [B] [C] [D]	18	[A] [B] [C] [D]
5	[A] [B] [C] [D]	12	[A] [B] [C] [D]	19	[A] [B] [C] [D]
6	[A] [B] [C] [D]	13	[A] [B] [C] [D]	20	[A] [B] [C] [D]
7	[A] [B] [C] [D]	14	[A] [B] [C] [D]		

Write below any questions you would like to ask your instructor about the lessons.

....

....

....

Now look over this student report answer sheet to be sure you have completed all the questions. Then return it to your GU instructor or office in your area. The address should be stamped on the copyright page near the front of your study guide.

For GU Office Use Only

Date .... Score ....

GU Christian Service Program

CS2221 *Tents, Temples, and Palaces*
UNIT TWO ANSWER SHEET

We hope you have enjoyed your study of the lessons in Unit 2! Please fill in all the blanks below.

Your Name ....

Your GU Student Number ....
(Leave blank if you do not know what it is.)

Your Mailing Address ....
....
City ....
Province/State .... Postal/Zip ....
Country ....

Answer Sheet for Unit Two

Blacken the correct space for each numbered item. For all questions, be sure the number beside the spaces on the answer sheet is the same as the number of the question.

1. [A] [B] [C] [D]
2. [A] [B] [C] [D]
3. [A] [B] [C] [D]
4. [A] [B] [C] [D]
5. [A] [B] [C] [D]
6. [A] [B] [C] [D]
7. [A] [B] [C] [D]
8. [A] [B] [C] [D]
9. [A] [B] [C] [D]
10. [A] [B] [C] [D]
11. [A] [B] [C] [D]
12. [A] [B] [C] [D]
13. [A] [B] [C] [D]
14. [A] [B] [C] [D]
15. [A] [B] [C] [D]
16. [A] [B] [C] [D]
17. [A] [B] [C] [D]
18. [A] [B] [C] [D]
19. [A] [B] [C] [D]
20. [A] [B] [C] [D]

Write below any questions you would like to ask your instructor about the lessons.

. . . .

. . . .

. . . .

Now look over this student report answer sheet to be sure you have completed all the questions. Then return it to your GU instructor or office in your area. The address should be stamped on the copyright page near the front of your study guide.

For GU Office Use Only

Date . . . . Score . . . .

GU Christian Service Program

CS2221   Tents, Temples, and Palaces
UNIT THREE ANSWER SHEET

We hope you have enjoyed your study of the lessons in Unit 3! Please fill in all the blanks below.

Your Name ....

Your GU Student Number ....
(Leave blank if you do not know what it is.)

Your Mailing Address ....

....

City ....

Province/State .... Postal/Zip ....

Country ....

ANSWER SHEET FOR UNIT THREE

Blacken the correct space for each numbered item. For all questions, be sure the number beside the spaces on the answer sheet is the same as the number of the question.

1	A	B	C	D	8	A	B	C	D	15	A	B	C	D
2	A	B	C	D	9	A	B	C	D	16	A	B	C	D
3	A	B	C	D	10	A	B	C	D	17	A	B	C	D
4	A	B	C	D	11	A	B	C	D	18	A	B	C	D
5	A	B	C	D	12	A	B	C	D	19	A	B	C	D
6	A	B	C	D	13	A	B	C	D	20	A	B	C	D
7	A	B	C	D	14	A	B	C	D					

Write below any questions you would like to ask your instructor about the lessons.

. . . .

. . . .

. . . .

Now look over this student report answer sheet to be sure you have completed all the questions. Then return it to your GU instructor or office in your area. The address should be stamped on the copyright page near the front of your study guide.

For GU Office Use Only

Date . . . . Score . . . .

GU Christian Service Program

CS2221   Tents, Temples, and Palaces

Your Name . . . .
Your GU Student Number . . . .
            (Leave blank if you do not know what it is.)
Your Mailing Address . . . .
. . . .
City . . . .
Province/State . . . .   Postal/Zip . . . .
Country . . . .

Answer Sheet for Unit Three

Blacken the correct space for each numbered item. For all questions, be sure the number beside the spaces on the answer sheet is the same as the number of the question.

1 A B C D	8 A B C D	15 A B C D
2 A B C D	9 A B C D	16 A B C D
3 A B C D	10 A B C D	17 A B C D
4 A B C D	11 A B C D	18 A B C D
5 A B C D	12 A B C D	19 A B C D
6 A B C D	13 A B C D	20 A B C D
7 A B C D	14 A B C D	

Write below any questions you would like to ask your instructor about the lessons.

....
....
....

Now look over this student report answer sheet to be sure you have completed all the questions. Then return it to your GU instructor or office in your area. The address should be stamped on the copyright page near the front of your study guide.

For GU Office Use Only

Date .... Score ....

GU Christian Service Program

Your Name ....

Your GU Student Number ....
       (Leave blank if you do not know what it is.)

Your Mailing Address ....

....

City ....

Province/State .... Postal/Zip ....

Country ....

REQUEST FOR INFORMATION

The GU office in your area will be happy to send you information about other GU courses that are available and their cost. You may use the space below to ask for that information.

....
....
....

INVITATION TO ACCEPT JESUS CHRIST AS LORD AND SAVIOR

Becoming a Christian and receiving the gift of eternal life is a choice you make. God has done everything possible to open the door to heaven for you. Jesus suffered a cruel death on the Cross, taking the punishment we rightfully deserved, so that the very worst of sinners can now be fully forgiven and receive the gift of eternal life.

To receive this gift, you need to admit that you are a sinner and ask God to forgive you of all the evil deeds you have done. You need to trust in and take Jesus Christ into your life as your Lord and Savior.

If you are ready to receive Jesus, say this prayer now and mean it from your heart:

> Dear Father in heaven, I recognize today that I have sinned against you, and it is my desire to turn away from my sins from this day forward. Please forgive me. I also believe You sent Your Son, Jesus Christ, to die in my place on the cross and that He rose from the dead on the third day. I receive Him today as my Lord and Savior by faith and will live for Him the rest of my life. Please change my life and make your presence known in me. I ask this in Jesus' holy name, Amen.

Please write in BLOCK letters:

Your Name:..

Post Office Box: ....

Street Address: ....

....

City: ....

State/Province: ....

Postal or Zip Code: ....

Country : ....

E-mail address: ....

1. *Were you a Christian, having understood God's plan of salvation and accepted Jesus as your Savior, before starting this course?* ....

2. *Did you accept Jesus Christ as a result of studying these lessons?* ....

3. *Do you belong to a local church?* .... *If so, what church?* ....

4. *Would you like to have an address of a local church in your area?* ....

5. *Would you like to have information about other courses like this that you can study?* ....

Congratulations on having finished this Christian Service course. Cut this sheet from your course and send it to your national Global University office if indicated or local church study center or Global University's international headquarters in Springfield, MO, USA (address shown on the back cover).

May God bless you as you love and serve Him.

SEND US THE NAMES AND ADDRESSES OF YOUR FRIENDS

We will send them Lesson 1 of our evangelism booklet "The Great Questions of Life."

Print Clearly

Last Name ....

First Name ....

Mailing Address ....

....

City ....

Province or State ....

Zip or Postal Code ....

Country ....

Last Name ....

First Name ....

Mailing Address ....

....

City ....

Province or State ....

Zip or Postal Code ....

Country ....

Last Name ....

First Name ....

Mailing Address ....

....

City ....

Province or State ....

Zip or Postal Code ....

Country ....

Last Name ....

First Name ....

Mailing Address ....

....

City ....

Province or State ....

Zip or Postal Code ....

Country ....
